BRUGES

GW00705997

APA PUBLICATIONS
Part of the Langenscheidt Publishing Group

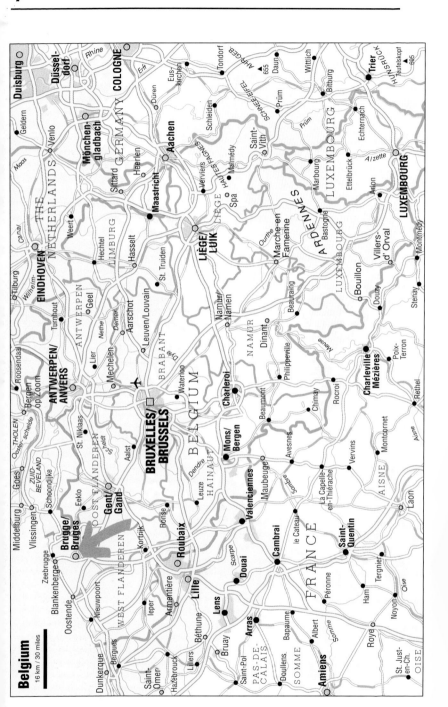

Belgium

16 km / 30 miles

Welcome

This guidebook combines the interests and enthusiasms of two of the world's best-known information providers: Insight Guides, who have set the standard for visual travel guides since 1970, and Discovery Channel, the world's premier source of non-fiction television programming. Its aim is to help you make the best of your stay in Bruges (Brugge), one of Europe's best-preserved medieval cities. Compared with some cities, Bruges is small and easy to get to grips with, which means it should not be unrealistic for you to see just about everything. To smooth the way through the city's tourist-thronged, cobbled streets, Insight Guides' correspondent in Bruges, George McDonald, has devised three itineraries linking the essential sights in the Old City – these are not quite day-long tours, giving you the option of squeezing in all or part of another tour on a long summer day. Six further itineraries open up other areas and aspects of the city. Four full-day excursions add other dimensions to a trip to Belgium's Flanders region. The first skips out of town to Damme, every bit as historic as Bruges but a lot smaller, and just 6km (4 miles) away – about the same as a moderate subway ride in New York, London or Paris. Then we take you to Ghent, that great rival of Bruges; to Ostend, the faded former Queen of the Coast; and to Ypres, the setting for some of the worst fighting of World War I.

George McDonald, a freelance travel writer, first came to Bruges on the train from Brussels, where he was living and working as editor of the in-flight magazine of the Belgian airline Sabena. Having learned Dutch (more or less) while living in Amsterdam, he thought he would have no problems in Dutch-speaking Bruges – or Brugge as its people call this canal-fretted city – but that was before he caught a whiff of the West Flanders accent. No matter, many people from Bruges speak excellent English – not to mention passable French, German, Spanish and other languages that bring tourist cash to town. George McDonald is also the author of *Insight Compact Guide: Bruges*, Insight Pocket Guides to Amsterdam and Brussels, and a contributor to Insight Guides to Belgium, the Netherlands, Brussels, Amsterdam and Cyprus.

HISTORY AND CULTURE

From its indistinct origins in the Dark Ages, through its heyday as a medieval trading centre, then centuries of civil and religious turmoil under foreign rule, Bruges was frequently at the forefront of art and architecture. All of this helped to shape the city we see today **11**

CITY ITINERARIES

The first three itineraries in this selection are full-day tours linking the city's highlights. They are followed by six shorter tours exploring other interesting areas and aspects of Bruges, away from the tourist hustle and bustle.

EXCURSIONS

These four excursions take you to destinations within easy reach of Bruges and include a book-buyer's paradise, a historic rival town, a busy port and seaside resort, and a brave little town with reminders of World War I.

LEISURE ACTIVITIES

CALENDAR OF EVENTS

PRACTICAL INFORMATION

MAPS

CREDITS AND INDEX

Pages 2/3: canal view from Potterierei
Pages 8/9: cyclist in Damme

History & Culture

Bruges begins to emerge indistinctly from the mists of the Dark Ages around the mid-7th century, when St Elegius preached in the coastal plain of Flanders. Chronicles of his life refer to a Frankish community called *municipium Flandrense*. This seems to have been Bruges (Elegius is sometimes credited with founding Holy Saviour's Church in 646), perhaps the vestiges of a Roman settlement, protected against raiding Germanic tribes by a *castellum* (fortress) as the Roman Empire went into its decline.

The first certain mention of Bruges occurs in 851 in records kept by monks from Ghent, and by 864 the word *Bruggia* appears on coins of the Frankish emperor Charles the Bald, to whom Flanders owed allegiance. Baldwin I (Iron Arm), whose residence was a castle in the Burg, is the first count of Flanders we know by name. He seems to have been a swashbuckler, eloping with Charles's daughter Judith and living to tell the tale.

The counts of Flanders gradually gained independence from France and survived until Count Louis of Male died in 1384. Along the way Count Charles the Good was murdered in St Donatian's Church in 1127 and a relic of Christ's blood arrived from the Holy Land, reputedly brought by Count Thierry of Alsace around 1149 – though it is more likely that it came in the time of Count Baldwin IX, the first Latin Emperor of Constantinople (1204–5) after the Fourth Crusade had captured the Byzantine capital and looted its treasures. You can see the relic in the Basilica of the Holy Blood.

City Defences and Medieval Architecture

Maritime trade and textiles manufacture brought prosperity to the growing town, which was protected by walls that had been thrown up around the inner canal circuit in the aftermath of Charles the Good's assassination. A second line of walls, whose outline is preserved in the ring canal and its park, was built during the 14th century. Four of the original nine city gates survive, powerful bulwarks that give an indication of the former strength of these moated defences.

The city's most important architectural works were begun during the medieval period. Highly visible Gothic symbols speak volumes about its civic pride. The Belfry soars above the Market Hall in the Markt, which was then the city's commercial heart. Politics held sway in the neighbouring Burg, with the magnificent Town Hall inspiring the efforts of other Belgian cities. St John's Hospital and the churches show that the religious authorities were determined not to be left behind, and neither were the builders of the private mansions and guildhouses.

Left: Gothic symbols represent civic pride
Right: custodian of a rich heritage

The Burgundy Dukes

After the demise of Count Louis of Male, Flanders passed to Duke Philip the Bold of the House of Burgundy through his marriage to Louis' daughter and heir. Philip eventually added most of the Low Countries to what had become his empire – and bequeathed the adjective 'Burgundian' to describe Belgium. The dynasty lasted nearly a century and included the memorably named John the Fearless, Philip the Good and Charles the Bold. Philip the Good built the Prinsenhof and in 1430 founded in Bruges the Order of the Golden Fleece, armorials of which you can see in Holy Saviour's Cathedral, St James's Church and the Church of Our Lady. Today's quinquennial Praalstoet van de Gouden Boom (Golden Tree Parade) recalls the sumptuous marriage of Charles the Bold to Margaret of York in 1468, when a grand tournament and procession was held in the Markt.

Charles the Bold proved too bold for his own good by challenging France, losing both the decisive Battle of Nancy and his life in 1477. Charles's daughter and heir, Mary of Burgundy, suffered a fatal fall from a horse in 1482 while hunting in the forest at Wijnendaele outside Bruges, which pitched Flanders into the hands of her husband, Crown Prince Maximilian of the Austrian House of Habsburg.

This period coincided with a great influx of wealth from textiles and trade. Bruges was a key member of the powerful Baltic-based Hanseatic League trading alliance, hosting the most important of the league's four principal *kontore* (foreign outposts).

Flemish Art

When, at the end of the 14th century, Bruges made the abrupt transition from the rule of the rough-and-ready counts of Flanders to that of the more sophisticated dukes of Burgundy, it was not long before art reflected the new regime's cosmopolitan tastes – art so significant that it influenced the early Renaissance artists of Italy. The first major artist to make his mark under Burgundian patronage was Jan van Eyck (*circa* 1390–1441). Probably born at Maaseyck (Maaseik) in Limburg, Van Eyck moved to Bruges in 1425, becoming court painter to Philip the Good.

Although he is credited with inventing oil painting, this is untrue. His use of oils was, however, revolutionary and he perfected the new medium, infusing subjects with an inner glow and surrounding them with symbolic meaning. He is the first of the 'Flemish Primitives', painters who broke from the rigid formalism of religious painting, showing a love of nature and portraying individuals realistically.

The Groeninge Museum has Van Eyck's *Madonna with Canon Joris van der Paele* (1436), a meticulously detailed altarpiece from St Donatian's Church, which shows St George 'presenting' Van der Paele to St Donatian while the Virgin Mary, with Christ on her knee, looks on approvingly. There is also a painting of his wife, *Portrait of Margareta van Eyck* (1439).

Petrus Christus (*circa* 1410–72), who was working in Bruges before 1440 and became a citizen in 1444, may have studied under Van Eyck. He continued in the footsteps of Van Eyck, both literally – by completing some of the master's unfinished works – and artistically, his own paintings being endowed with a more emotional tone.

Hans Memling (*circa* 1430–94), born in Germany, had a cool, poetic style that has given him a less dazzling reputation than the more popular masters. Most of his works are in the Memling Museum, including his *Triptych of St John* (1479), *Adoration of the Magi* (1479), and *Shrine of St Ursula* (1489). The Groeninge Museum exhibits his *Moreel Triptych* (1484). After Memling, Gerard David (*circa* 1460–1523), from Oudewater in Holland, was the most important artist working in Bruges and is considered the last of the Flemish Primitives. You can see his dramatic *Judgement of Cambyses* (1498), which was commissioned for the Town Hall council chamber, in the Groeninge Museum.

Around this time, wealthy individuals and trade guilds were beginning to build almshouses as refuges for the old, the poor and widows. The motivation was a composite of religious duty, guilty conscience and insurance against unrest. Having the grateful occupants pray twice daily in the almshouse chapel for their benefactor's soul was one way to help balance Heaven's books in their favour. Most almhouses now house senior citizens.

An End to Prosperity

Bruges was northwest Europe's economic capital from 1200 to 1400 and a major player in the 1500s. When the Zwin inlet silted up in the 1520s, cutting off Bruges' outlet to the sea, the encroaching sands choked its pros-

Left: Philip the Bold marries Margarete of Flanders
Above: Hans Memling's *Madonna with Child*

perity. Politics, however, dealt the final blow. After Bruges rebelled against the Habsburg Crown Prince Maximilian in 1482, locking him up and beheading his counsellor Pieter Lanchals, the empire struck back by replacing Bruges as its local capital with Ghent and transferring the city's trading privileges to Antwerp. Since Lanchals' family emblem was a swan, Maximilian also obliged the city to keep swans in its canals for ever, and Bruges is clearly still repaying this part of its debt.

Maximilian's son Philip the Fair married Joan the Mad, Queen of Castile, retaining the tradition of bizarre monikers and bringing Spain into the Habsburg fold.

The high point for Flanders was when Charles V, born in Ghent, inherited the Holy Roman Empire in 1516. Charles had visited Bruges in 1515, the same year that England's Thomas More met the humanist Erasmus in the city while on a diplomatic mission for Henry VIII, beginning an intellectual association that influenced his *Utopia*.

Bruges was past its economic prime when the Renaissance began to infiltrate in the baggage of Italian traders. The oldest Renaissance facade belongs to the Civic Registry in the Burg, which dates from 1534–7, though an interesting earlier (1460s) variation is the Florentine courtyard of Hof Bladelin.

With the Renaissance, the artistic focus in Flanders switched from Bruges to Antwerp. Nevertheless, artists like Jan Provoost from Mons, Adriaan Isenbrant from Haarlem, and Ambrosius Benson from Lombardy still worked in Bruges. Pieter Pourbus (*circa* 1523–84) from Gouda in Holland, who settled in the city, was one of the leading Renaissance painters in the Low Countries. Look for his *Portrait of Jan van Eyewerve* and *Portrait of Jacquemyne Buuk* (both 1551) in the Groeninge Museum. And you can see a highlight of Renaissance sculpture, Michelangelo's *Madonna and Child* (1505), in the Church of Our Lady.

Reformation and Revolution

After Charles V, Spain's heavy-handed Philip II, a fanatical Catholic, ruled the Low Countries, at a time when the Protestant Reformation was in full swing. The Jesuits, shock-troops of the Catholic Counter-Reformation, were active in Bruges, where the Calvinists had been strong enough to seize control of the city council for six years from 1578. They executed or chased away its monks and nuns, and after Spanish troops crushed the rebels in 1584, the Jesuits took up residence in Sint-Maartensplein, building a monastery, a college and a church, now St Walburga's. The savage suppression of Protestantism and rebellion in the southern Low Countries during the late 16th and early 17th centuries set the seal on economic collapse. Despite a Catholic resurgence, the first bishop of Bruges was not installed until 1662.

Just as in the Renaissance, Bruges' baroque artists were overshadowed by those of Antwerp. Works by Jacob van Oost (1601–71), Jan Baptist van Meunickxhoven (1620–1704), and the rococo artist Jan Garemijn (1712–99) can be seen in churches and in the Groeninge Museum. On the streets are sculptures by Pieter Peper, including a rococo pump (1761) in Eiermarkt and a statue of St John Nepomucene (1767) on the Sint-Jan Nepomucenus Bridge. Baroque architecture made a slightly better showing. The church of St Walburga (1619–43), designed by a Jesuit priest, is the finest example. Then there is the Provost's House in the Burg (1665–6), and the interiors of St Anne's Church and the church of Our Lady of the Pottery. Among many fine neoclassical buildings is the Palace of the Liberty of Bruges from 1722–7.

The Revolutionary French occupied Bruges in 1794 and seem to have spent most of the next 20 years knocking down churches, monasteries and palaces, along with much else of the Habsburg regime's feudal apparatus. In mitigation, most of the people of Bruges were thoroughly disillusioned with corrupt clerics and venal aristocrats and gave the demolition their enthusiastic support. The Napoleonic French were ejected in 1814 and Bruges became part of the Kingdom of the Netherlands. Far from popular, the Dutch held on until Belgium won its War of Independence in 1830. About the only noteworthy item from this period is the neoclassical Fish Market.

The Industrial Revolution mostly passed Bruges by, and it was a quaint, impoverished backwater by the time Belgium won independence. Not until the harbour at Zeebrugge was completed in 1904 and connected to Bruges by canal did the local economy again show signs of life – proof that prosperity was linked to maritime trade. By the end of the 19th century, Gothic style was back in vogue in Bruges: the Provincial House from 1887–92 in the Markt is a good example.

Literary Revival

In literature, the 19th century saw something of a flourish. Hendrik Conscience's novel *De Leeuw van Vlaanderen (The Lion of Flanders,* 1838) re-examined the heroic, Bruges-inspired revolt against the French in 1302, when a Flemish peasant army slaughtered the flower of French chivalry at the Battle of the Golden Spurs. Georges Rodenbach's famous novel *Bruges-la-Morte (Dead Bruges,* 1892) resonates with the air of mystery and decay into which Bruges had inexorably fallen after its golden age. Charles de Coster's *The Glorious Adventures of Tijl Uilenspiegel* (1867) gave neighbouring Damme its legendary local hero.

Right: the novelist Georges Rodenbach
Next Page: Bruges still attracts artists

A literary movement all by himself, the Catholic priest Guido Gezelle (1830–99) breathed new life into Flemish poetry with his volume *Kerkhof-blommen* (*Graveyard Flowers,* 1858), a mixture of literary Dutch and West Flanders dialect. Gezelle's ideas and nationalistic beliefs brought the Bruges-born cleric into conflict with the Church and educational authorities, and he abandoned poetry in the 1870s in favour of essays and translations. He returned to his first love in *Tijdkrans* (*Time's Garland,* 1893) and *Rijms-noer* (*String of Rhymes,* 1897), poems dealing with nature, religion and Flemish nationalism that show an original use of rhyme, metaphor and sound. A founder-member of the Flemish Academy of Language, he spent much of his career teaching and as a parish priest in Kortrijk, but returned to Bruges in the last year of his life as rector of the English Convent. His work is available in English in *Poems/Gedichten* (1972).

Preserving the City

Bruges counts only three examples – a shopfront, a restaurant and a house facade – of the Art Nouveau style that made such a big impact elsewhere in turn-of-the-20th-century Europe. Art Deco does even worse, its only notable example an office building that houses the Dutch Consulate.

Since World War II, tourism has been the main engine of prosperity, but its architectural heritage was in poor and declining shape until well into the 1960s. Gothic buildings need plenty of expensive upkeep, and the process of stabilising the 'look' of Bruges is still going on. Though much of the heavy lifting has been done, there are still buildings that look in imminent danger of collapse and, getting right down to basics, the sewerage system can also add – though in a less agreeable way – to the city's atmosphere.

Constant refurbishment has given the city an almost unreal quality. A place that looks and feels like a museum can be hard to get close to, how-ever grateful we might be that it has come safely down the centuries. Yet there is nowhere quite like Bruges. Its Gothic buildings, gabled houses, meandering canals, and cobbled streets form a whole that is undeniably romantic. Phrases such as the 'Venice of the North' or 'Belgium's Ams-terdam' do the city no service: Bruges is no imitation and needs no such comparisons to illuminate its unique qualities.

HISTORY HIGHLIGHTS

1st century AD Gallo-Roman settlement founded. It has trading links with Gaul and Britain

851 First known mention of Bruges.

863 Baldwin I 'Iron Arm', the first count of Flanders to be known by name, occupies the castle in the Burg.

circa 940 Count Arnulf I builds Church of St Donatian.

11th century Role of maritime trading centre comes to an end when silting closes access to sea.

1127 First town charter. Building begins on the city walls.

1134 Flood creates Zwin inlet between sea and Damme; canal to Damme reopens maritime trade.

circa 1149 Count Thierry of Alsace is said to bring relic of Holy Blood from Jerusalem.

1157 St Basil's Church, later Basilica of the Holy Blood, completed.

13th century Belfry, Hallen, Begijnhof and St Jan's Hospital begun.

1297 France's King Philip IV annexes Flanders.

1302 Pieter De Coninck and Jan Breidel lead rebellion; Flemish peasants and craftsmen slaughter French knights at Battle of the Golden Spurs.

1376 Work begins on Town Hall.

1384 Margaret, wife of Burgundy's Duke Philip the Bold, succeeds to throne of Flanders.

1436 Van Eyck paints *Virgin and Child*.

1436–8 Failed rebellion against Duke Philip the Good.

1474–9 Hans Memling paints *Triptych of St John*.

1477 Death of Duke Charles the Bold sparks rebellion. Mary of Burgundy, wife of Habsburg Maximilian of Austria, inherits throne.

1488 Bruges rebels; Maximilian transfers ducal seat to Ghent.

1506 Jan van Mouskroen brings Michelangelo's *Madonna and Child* from Italy to Church of Our Lady.

1520 Silting closes Zwin outlet.

1527 Hendrik van Dommele, city's first Protestant martyr, burned at stake.

1559 Bishopric of Bruges established.

1577 Bruges joins Low Countries rebellion against Spain.

1581 Protestantism becomes the only permitted religion.

1584–5 Spain re-establishes control. Protestant merchants, artists and craftsmen flee to Netherlands. Bruges enters steep decline.

1622 Ostend canal restores Bruges' outlet to the sea.

1782–4 Austrian emperor dismantles walls, closes monasteries.

1794–5 Revolutionary France annexes Bruges. Many churches and monasteries destroyed.

1815 Napoleon defeated at Waterloo. Bruges becomes part of Netherlands.

1830–31 Bruges joins Southern Netherlands revolt against Dutch, becoming part of Belgium.

1847 Hunger riots take place in Belgium's poorest city.

1892 George Rodenbach's novel *Bruges-la-Morte* published.

1899 Poet Guido Gezelle dies.

1904 Zeebrugge harbour completed.

1914–18 World War I. The Germans occupy Bruges.

1939–45 World War II. The Germans occupy Bruges from 1940–44.

1950s Tourist boom begins.

1971 A merger with neighbouring municipalities creates third-largest city in Flanders.

2000 The city co-hosts the Euro 2000 soccer finals.

2002 Bruges is one of the Cultural Capitals of Europe.

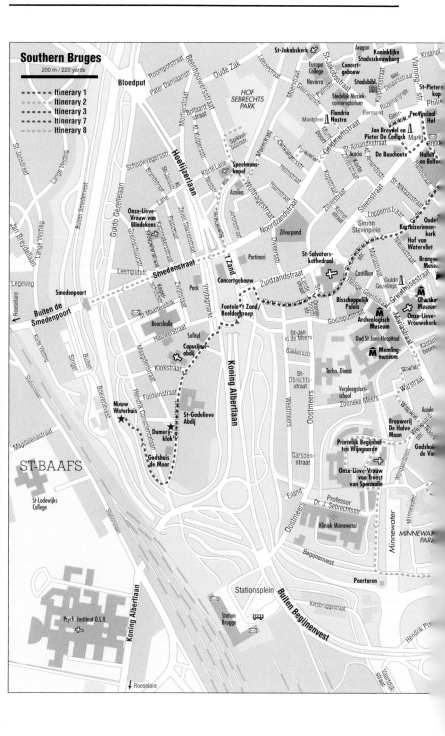

Southern Bruges

200 m / 220 yards

- Itinerary 1
- Itinerary 2
- Itinerary 3
- Itinerary 7
- Itinerary 8

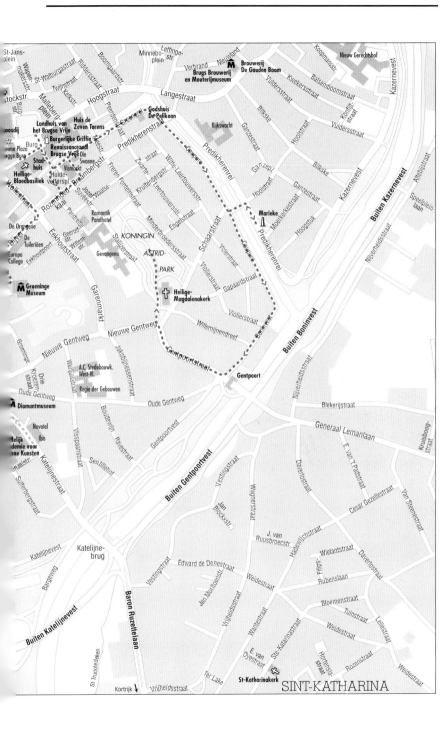

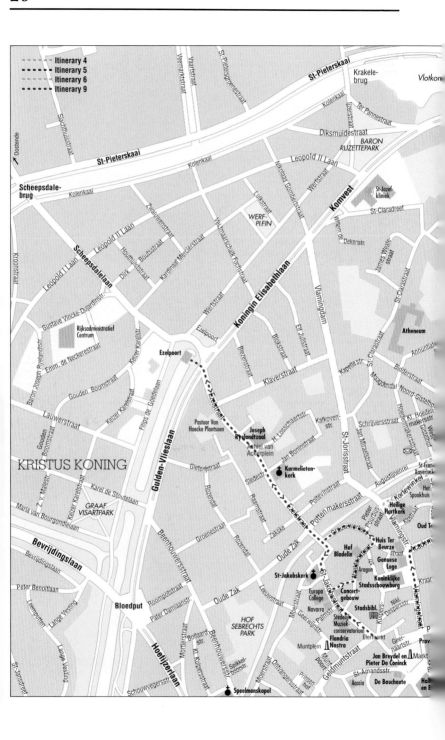

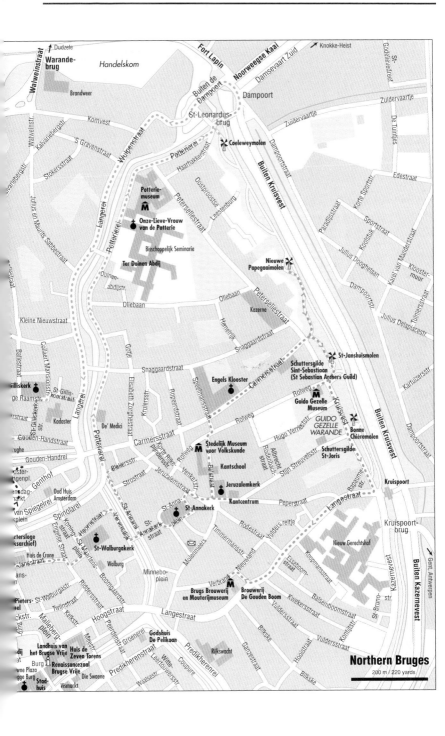

Northern Bruges

200 m / 220 yards

City
Itineraries

B ruges has 120,000 inhabitants, 50,000 of whom live in the old city within the ring canal. The heart of the city is small and, thanks to vigorous anti-traffic measures, it is easily navigated on foot, so even on a tight schedule you can see a lot. And don't forget that this is not really 'Bruges' at all – but Brugge. Just below the cosmopolitan surface with which it greets you, Bruges is the pride and joy of Dutch-speaking Flanders, Flemish with heart and soul. To get below the surface you need to remember this.

Almost all the itineraries commence on or near the Markt and the Burg, two monumental squares in the centre of town. They then fan out to all points of the compass. The first three full-day itineraries get you around many of the city's highlights. After that you will be able to cherry-pick from the shorter tours. Don't be afraid to jump from one itinerary to a neighbouring one; check the tour maps and you will see that often there are connecting points where you can do this without any trouble. A little advance planning will take you a long way.

Bruges rewards aimless wandering as well as itinerary-following, so try to set aside some time for just strolling around (or taking a canal-boat trip), with eyes open and guidebook closed, making your own discoveries. Walking gets you closer to the legacy of a thousand years of history in one of Europe's most picturesque cities.

1. THE HEART OF BRUGES *(see map, p18–19)*

A turn around the city's majestic market square and a climb to the top of its soaring Belfry, followed by a stroll along the central canal and visits to the Brangwyn and Groeninge museums and a restored 15th-century palace, add up to a six-hour tour through the heart of Bruges.

To the start: You can't easily miss the Markt, since its flat-topped Belfry is a prominent landmark for miles around. If you are coming from the railway station, take De Lijn city buses 1, 3, 4, 6, 8, 11, 13 or 16 from Stationsplein. Or walk the 1.5km (1 mile) along Oostmeers and Steenstraat.

The venerable facades of the **Markt** (Market Square) at the city's medieval heart make this among the finest squares in the Low Countries, though most of its gabled houses have been turned into restaurants and cafes. (The Markt lives up to its name by hosting a street market every Wednesday morning.) A heroic sculpture from 1887 in the centre honours two local heroes, butcher Jan Breydel and weaver Pieter De Coninck, who in 1302 inspired the Bruges Matins revolt against the occupying French. As a result of their action, later that year

Left: Market Square is one of the finest in the Low Countries
Right: heroes from 1302 are honoured in the square's centre

a ragtag band of Flemish rebels annihilated an army of French knights at the Battle of the Golden Spurs, near Kortrijk.

The sculpture is a good place from which to take in the soaring Gothic **Belfort** (Belfry; tel: 050-874411; Tues–Sun 9.30am–5pm), 88m (290ft) high and tilting 1.2m (4ft) from the vertical at its summit. Rising out of the Hallen *(see opposite)*, the Belfry was intended to be a highly visible symbol of civic pride. The stone tower's lower half dates from 1296 and the octagonal lantern from 1487. These replaced an earlier wooden tower that burned down in 1280, driving the city aldermen, who met in a Belfry chamber, away to a new seat in the Burg *(see Itinerary 3, page 33)*. A wooden spire crowned the structure, as you can see in old prints such as Marcus Gerard's engraved 1562 *Map of Bruges*, but it burned down in 1493 and the same fate befell a replacement in 1741, leaving the tower, tall as it is, with a somewhat truncated look.

If you have the stamina for it, climb the Belfry's 366 steps inside a steep, narrow stairwell. These take you past the second-floor **Treasury**, where the medieval town's seal and charters were kept in a wooden chest secured by seven locks, behind an iron grille with a lock opened by nine keys. Continue upwards to reach the impressive clock mechanism from 1680 and a 47-bell carillon weighing 27 tonnes, which chimes a folk tune every 15 minutes. It is served by a full-time *carilloneur* who climbs up here three times a week to perform concerts. At the top a windswept observation platform gives a panoramic view of the city and the West Flanders polderland stretching away to the sea.

Above: cafés abound around Market Square
Left: the Belfry is Bruges' own leaning tower

Merchants' Hall

The vast **Hallen** (Market Hall) from which the Belfry rises dates princi-
pally from 1240 to the 15th century, with later additions, and it replaced an
earlier wooden structure. Originally used by cloth merchants, its four wings
surrounding a central courtyard lined with galleries were for centuries a
focal point of the city's commercial life. In recent years, the Adornes con-
sortium of local art dealers has brought it back into use as a commercial
and exhibition centre. In front of the Hallen is a miniature bronze replica
of the Belfry and Hallen, with information inscribed in Braille. The southern wing's Renaissance galleries, facing Oude Burg, occasionally host special
events. To gain access to the Belfry entrance, pass through an arched entrance
in the Markt to the interior courtyard.

Circle the Markt to pick out other points of interest. The group of three
ornate buildings on the eastern side is a prime example of how Bruges plays
visual tricks that throw your sense of time out of joint. Except for its over-
elaborate tracery, the **Provinciaal Hof** (Provincial House) looks just like a
contemporary of the Hallen. In fact this government seat of West Flanders
Province dates from 1887–1921 and is neo-Gothic – fake Gothic, you might
say. Flanking it, the post office building and the offices of the Vlaamse
Gemeenschap (Flemish Community) are also architectural deceptions.

Should you want to have lunch or dinner, **La Civière d'Or** at No 33, in
the former Fishmongers' Guildhouse, is a good spot. At No 16, the **Craenenburg**, a turreted, crenellated mansion with stained-glass windows that houses
an authentic Flemish cafe/restaurant, was in the Middle Ages a residence
of knights of the Count of Flanders and their ladyfolk. In 1488, the citizens
imprisoned Crown Prince Maximilian of Austria here for 100 days after
the Habsburg authorities had imposed new taxes. Facing the Craenenburg,
across Sint-Amandstraat at Markt
15, **De Bouchoute** from around
1480, hosted Britain's exiled King
Charles II in 1656–7.

To the Martyr's Bridge

Take busy Wollestraat, a shopping
street at the southeast corner of the
Markt, beside the Hallen, and follow it to its end. In the loggia of the
lace shop at No 9 a 'little old lady'
works unceasingly on her lace.
Three reliefs on the facade of No
28 show scenes from the 1631 siege
of Bruges by the Protestant Dutch
army of Prince Frederik Henry of
Orange. Take the narrow side lane
opposite to reach a scenic waterside
viewpoint situated between the
classic restaurants, 't Bourgoensche
Cruyce and Bourgoensch Hof. Back

Right: one way to see the sights

on Wollestraat, just before the bridge over the Reie, the ornate **De Malvenda House** at No 53 was the home of 16th-century Spanish magistrate Juan Pérez de Malvenda.

The bridge ahead of you is the **Sint-Jan Nepomucenusbrug**, which is graced with a statue dating from 1767 of the Bohemian martyr St John Nepomucene (*circa* 1345–93), the patron saint of the Czech Republic and of bridges. Standing between two wrought-iron lamps, the saint is depicted with a forlorn expression, as though he were about to be pitched into the water – which is precisely how he was martyred, drowned in the River Vltava. From

the jetty to the right of the bridge you can embark upon canal-boat tours.

Turn right along the canal to **Dijver**, a tree-shaded quay lined with mostly neoclassical buildings, where a weekend antiques and flea market takes place between mid-March and mid-November. Across the water you can see the back of the former Carthusian Convent and the orangery behind the 19th-century De Halleux House in Oude Burg (*see Itinerary 7, page 46*). At No 11, the **Europa College**, which opened in 1949, hosts postgraduate students from around the world who come here to study the European Union's political, economic and legal affairs.

The Groeninge Museum

At No 12, turn left along a pathway to the **Stedelijk Museum voor Schone Kunsten** (Municipal Fine Arts Museum), more commonly known as the **Groeninge Museum** (tel: 050-448711; Tues–Sun 9.30am–5pm). Opened in 1930 on the site of a former Augustinian monastery, the Groeninge houses a superb collection of works by the 15th-century 'Flemish Primitives', who, as the free audio guide informs you, were far from being primitive. They were, in fact, responsible for a revolutionary step forward in art by moving away from rigidly religious themes and depicting real people in their paintings.

On display in this splendid setting are remarkable works that seem to bring the medieval world to life. They include Jan van Eyck's *Madonna with Canon Joris van der Paele* (1436) and *Portrait of Margereta van Eyck* (1439), depicting his wife at 33; Hans Memling's *Moreel Triptych* (the *Triptych with St Christopher*, 1484); *Death of the Virgin* (*circa* 1470) by Hugo van der Goes; and works by Rogier van der Weyden, Pieter Pourbus, Petrus Christus, Gerard David, Pieter Brueghel the Elder and the Younger, and others. Another important painting is *The Last Judgement* (*circa* 1500) by Hieronymous Bosch, a grim account of the trials that await sinners in the afterlife. Two other nonchalantly gruesome works are the *Judgement of Cambyses* (1498) by Gerard David, showing the corrupt Persian judge being flayed alive by industrious torturers, and the *Martyrdom of St Hippolytus*

Above: Bohemian martyr St John Nepomucene, patron saint of bridges

(circa 1468), a triptych by Dieric Bouts and Hugo van der Goes, in which the saint is being torn apart by four horses. Also, don't ignore less-advertised paintings such as *The Town Docks at Bruges* (1653) by Hendrik van Minderhout, which gives an idea of the size of the merchant ships that routinely called at Bruges. There are also modern works by Jean Delville, Rik Wouters, René Magritte, Paul Delvaux and others.

Art and Lace

Cross the Groeninge lane into **Hof Arents** (Arents Park), formerly the gardens of Gruuthuse Palace *(see below),* passing a modern sculpture group, the *Four Horsemen of the Apocalypse*, representing the horrors of war, death, famine and revolution, and two columns that are all that survive of the Waterhalle, a building that until 1786 stood in the Markt. This brings you to a late 18th-century mansion, the **Arentshuis**, home to the **Brangwyn Museum** (tel: 050-448711; Tues–Sun 9.30am–5pm), dedicated to the works of British artist Frank Brangwyn (1867–1956), who was born in Bruges and who returned to paint and sketch the town. His oil paintings, watercolours, etchings and tapestries are on the first floor. On the ground floor, the **Lace Museum** (same opening times as Brangwyn Museum), holds a selection of lace from various city collections, illustrating the use of lace as costume decoration over the centuries.

The Gruuthuse Palace

Go back through Arents Park, under a double archway at the end, and across the narrow, pretty little **Bonifatiusbrug** (Boniface Bridge), noting the tiny, timber-faced canalside houses to your left, and passing a statue of the Spanish-born humanist philosopher Juan Luis Vivés (1492–1540), an associate of Erasmus and Thomas More.

Above: the excellent Groeninge Museum
Left: one of the *Four Horsemen of the Apocalypse*

You come now to the lavish, restored 15th-century **Paleis van de Heeren van Gruut-huse** (Palace of the Lords of Gruuthuse), seat of a family who had a monopoly on the sale of *gruut,* a herbal mixture for improving the flavour of beer, and who later owned the beer tax concession. The family's leading light, Lodewijk van Gruuthuse *(circa* 1427–92), was a counsellor to the Burgundian dukes Philip the Good and Charles the Bold. His equestrian statue stands above the entrance to his Burgundian abode, a fantastic Gothic tracery of rose-coloured stone with high towers and arched windows (though largely a late

19th-century reconstruction). It was refuge for two exiled English kings – Edward IV in 1470–71 and Charles II in 1656.

The palace houses the **Gruuthuse Museum** (tel: 050-448711; Tues–Sun 9.30am–5pm), containing artefacts, decorative arts and treasures that represent life in 15th- and 16th-century Bruges – at least as it was lived by the high and mighty. There are some 2,500 objects, among them paintings, sculptures, musical instruments, lace, silk, tapestries, furniture, weapons and glassware. In one room is a terracotta bust from around 1520, with later polychrome and wood additions, of Emperor Charles V as an optimistic young man of 20, before the cares of war, religious strife and political intrigue had worn him down. You can kneel in Lodewijk van Gruuthuse's oak-panelled Gothic oratory from 1472, a private chapel that butted into the adjacent Church of Our Lady *(see Itinerary 2, page 29)*, giving him and his family an undisturbed, overhead view of the altar. The Gruuthuse family's aposite motto, *Plus Est En Vous* (There Is More In You), is inscribed on the balustrade above an arch in the ornate reception hall.

The mansion's former stables in the courtyard now house a cafeteria, but the **Maria van Boergondië** restaurant at 1 Guido Gezelleplein is a better place to recover from your exertions.

2. ARTISTIC HERITAGE AND
THE LAKE OF LOVE *(see map, p18–19)*

This six-hour itinerary begins in a square named after the city's premier literary figure, moves on to a church graced with a Michelangelo sculpture and a museum dedicated to a great artist, followed by a pause for a beer at a traditional brewery, before continuing to the tranquil Béguinage and the scenic Lake of Love.

To the start: Take De Lijn city bus 1 to Mariastraat, from where the starting point is no more than a few metres.

In the square called **Guido Gezelleplein** stands a statue, erected in 1930, of the Bruges poet-priest Guido Gezelle (1830–99), one of the most notable Flemish men of letters, wearing a suitably solemn expression. Sidestep a short distance to Heilige Geeststraat and you arrive at the **Archeologisch Museum** (Archaeological Museum; tel: 050-448711; Tues–Sun 9.30am–12.30pm and 1.30–5pm), in the former eye clinic of Sint-Janshospitaal *(see page 30)*, to view its small but interesting collection of pottery, glass, leather, stone figurines and tomb paintings.

The Church of Our Lady

Across the way on Mariastraat, the colossal **Onze-Lieve-Vrouwekerk** (Church of Our Lady; Mon–Sat 10–11.30am and 2.30–5pm, Sun 2.30–4pm) was first mentioned in written records in 1089, though by then the church was already two centuries old. The church's 122m (395ft) brick spire is an even more visible city landmark than that of the Belfry in the Markt and is said to be the world's highest brick tower.

Inside is where the 13th- to 15th-century church's true glories are. First among those treasures is the *Madonna and Child* by Michelangelo *(see picture on page 30)*, created in 1504–5 for the cathedral of Siena, which couldn't afford to pay for it. A wealthy Bruges merchant, Jan van Mouskroen, bought the statue in 1506 and donated it to Our Lady's in 1514. The only one of Michelangelo's works to leave Italy during the artist's life, the statue remains one of only a few that can be seen outside Italy. The proportions of the smallish Carrara marble sculpture, kept behind protective glass in a side chapel, suggest it was designed to be viewed from a lower angle than its present situation allows.

During the Burgundian period, this was the royal chapel of the Dukes of Burgundy. Here, in a lavish ceremony in 1477, Mary of Burgundy, daughter of Charles the Bold, married Maximilian of Austria, Crown Prince of the Habsburg Empire (though neither bride nor groom could speak the other's language). In the choir you can see the magnificent side-by-side tombs of Charles the Bold, who was killed at the Battle of Nancy in 1477, and of Mary, who died in a riding accident in 1482 at the age of 25. Mary's sarcophagus, made from black marble surmounted by a graceful, reclining image of her in gilded bronze, dates from 1502 and is a superb example of late Gothic art.

Above Left: exhibit at the Lace Museum. **Left:** Boniface Bridge
Right: Flemish poet and priest Guido Gezelle

Charles the Bold's tomb – there's an element of doubt about whether the remains inside really are his – also has a recumbent image of the deceased in bronze, but it was not completed until the mid-16th century, by which time the Renaissance style was in vogue.

There are a number of other notable memorials in the church, including the funerary chapel of Pieter Lanchals, Maximilian of Austria's assassinated counsellor, with a painting of *Our Lady of the Seven Sorrows (circa* 1520) by Adrian Isenbrandt. There is also a *Crucifixion* (1626) by Antoon van Dyck, along with works by Dirk Bouts and Hugo van der Goes, plus a complete set of escutcheons of the Knights of the Golden Fleece, who

held a chapter meeting in Our Lady's in 1468. Back outside, in Onze-Lieve-Vrouwekerkhof-Zuid at the side of the church, look for the house dating from 1904 at Nos 6–8, which has a pink Art Nouveau façade with murals representing Day and Night.

The Memling Collection

Back on Mariastraat, continue to the former **Sint-Janshospitaal** (St John's Hospital), which was a work-in-progress from the 12th to 17th centuries. Three of its wards and its Romanesque tower were built in the early 1200s, and two more wards were added in the late 1300s. The huge complex inside the 13th-century façade is now divided between an arts and a congress centre, and its grounds are a restful place for a stroll. In the cloisters near the entrance is a 17th-century apothecary. Pride of place, though, goes to the **Memling Museum** (tel: 050-448711; daily 9.30am–5pm; closed Wed Oct–Mar), in the hospital's church. It contains the greatest works of German-

born artist Hans Memling *(circa* 1440–94), who lived in Bruges from 1465 until his death, and a rich collection of religious vessels and sculpture. Memling works on display include the *Shrine of St Ursula (circa* 1489), a gilded wood reliquary in the shape of a Gothic church, on whose panels he painted scenes from the life of St Ursula, including her martyrdom by the Huns at Cologne, along with 11,000 virgins who had set out with her on a pilgrimage to Rome. Other highlights include the *Mystic Triptych*

Top: *Madonna and Child*, one of the few works by Michelangelo exhibited outside Italy
Above: mural at 6-8 Onze-Lieve-Vrouwekerkhof-Zuid. **Right:** taking a break

of St John (1474–9), part of an altarpiece that has side-panel images of John the Baptist and John the Evangelist, and the *Adoration of the Magi* (late 16th century) notable for its serene image of the Virgin Mary.

Almshouses and a Brewery Tour

Then, back on Katelijnestraat, on the right side of the street, is an entrance to the **Spanoghe Almshouse**, which was built in 1680. You get a better view of this by turning right a few steps further along and squeezing through narrow, dogleg Stoofstraat. Here a public bathhouse for both men and women basked in a steamy reputation, until the city authorities decided that cleanliness and godliness didn't mix after all, and closed it.

You now enter Walplein, a square with a modern sculpture of a bowler-hatted Zeus and a naked Leda, on a truly mythological visit to Bruges, being whisked along in an open carriage by the winged horse Pegasus. Across the square, through the courtyard of an old house at No 26, **Brouwerij De Halve Maan** (Apr–Oct: tours every hour Mon–Fri 11am–4pm, Sat–Sun 11am–5pm; Nov–Mar: tours daily at 11am and 3pm; www.halvemaan.be), in the former Henri Maes Brewery, has a brewing tradition that dates back to 1546 and today produces strapping blond Straffe Hendrik beer, which you can sample in the brewery's brasserie and in bars around town.

Cross Wijngaardstraat into Noordstraat, to **Godshuis de Vos**, an almshouse from 1713 on the right side of the street. This cluster of tiny whitewashed houses around a chapel is secluded behind its wall, but you can see into the enchanting courtyard garden, with its six little houses.

Pious Women of Bruges

Spirituality of a traditional kind is even more in evidence a short way off. Go back into Wijngaardstraat, then left over the bridge spanning the Reie, and through a neoclassical gateway, dated 1776, to reach the **Prinselijk Begijnhof ten Wijngaarde** (Princely Beguinage of the Vineyard), which derives its royal title from the fact that in 1299 France's King Philip IV placed it under his patronage. Founded in 1245 by Margaret of Constantinople, Countess of Flanders, though most of its present buildings date from the 17th century, this tranquil refuge continued into the 20th century as a home for *begijns,* religious women who performed a similar role to nuns. They took

no vows, but they lived an industrious and pious life caring for the sick or making lace. The *begijns* having died out, the Begijnhof has been a Benedictine convent since 1927, and the nuns now living there maintain many of its traditions.

Stroll around the cloister garden, dotted with poplar trees and a blaze of floral colour during spring and summer. You can visit the **Begijnhuisje**, one of the *begijns'* small whitewashed cottages (daily sunrise–sunset), still essentially in its 17th-century condition. You can also enter inside the Begijnhof church, **Onze-Lieve-Vrouw van Troost van Spermalie** (Our Lady of Consolation of Spermalie), but only if you wish to join the nuns in one of their regular services.

The Lake of Love

Leave by the Begijnhof's southern exit and turn left to the bridge, where you come to the old **Sashuis** (Lockkeeper's House). This stands beside a long rectangular stretch of water, the **Minnewater** (Lake of Love) – the name might be a felicitous modification of *Binnen Water* (Inner Harbour), where up to 150 seagoing ships and canal barges a day would have tied up during Bruges' 13th-century heyday as a member of the Hanseatic League. Stroll along the Minnewater's western bank to the **Poertoren** (Powder Tower); from 1398, the surviving one of two harbour defence towers (named after the gunpowder once stored there).

Beyond this is the beginning of the **Gentse Vaart** (Ghent Canal). Cross the bridge over the Minnewater into leafy **Minnewater Park**, where 19th-century **Kasteel Minnewater** (Minnewater Castle) houses a château-style restaurant, noted for seafood, with a waterside terrace.

Now walk along Arsenaalstraat – you pass a restored 16th-century chimney-tower and oven-vault in Noordstraat on the way – and turn left into Katelijnestraat, to reach the Stedelijk Academie voor Schone Kunsten (Municipal Fine Arts Academy) at No 86. It occupies the former monastery

Above: the Princely Beguinage of the Vineyard accommodated *begijns* until the 20th century

of the *beghards*, male equivalents of *begijns*, who were established here during the 13th century. It became a school for poor children in 1513 and took up its present use in 1891.

Further along Katelijnestraat you reach the **Diamantmuseum** (Diamond Museum; tel: 050-342056; daily 10.30am–5.30pm; www.diamondmuseum. be), which focuses on the history of diamond polishing in Bruges. The technique of using diamond powder on a rotating disk may have been invented by Bruges goldsmith Lodewijk van Berquen around 1476 and diamonds have been an important industry for the city at various periods during its history. In addition to offering diamond-polishing demonstrations, the museum displays tools, equipment and archival material.

3. THE BURG AND BEYOND *(see map, p18–19)*

A six-hour tour beginning with a stroll round one of the city's two majestic main squares, packed with historic sights such as the Palace of the Liberty of Bruges and the Basilica of the Holy Blood. From here you move on to a residential neighbourhood that provides a good comparison with the tourist zones.

To the start: Take De Lijn city buses 1, 3, 4, 6, 8, 11, 13 or 16 to the Markt, then walk along Breidelstraat to the Burg.

Around the cobbled **Burg** square, a harmonious array of monumental buildings spans the centuries from the 12th to the 19th, with architectural styles from Romanesque to postmodern. By the mid-9th century, the Franks had built a moated palisade or *burcht* here to protect it against Viking marauders. The fort has long since vanished, as has the castle of the counts of Flanders that replaced it.

As you enter the Burg on Breidelstraat, to your left is the ornately decorated **Proosdij** (Provost's House), rebuilt in baroque style in 1665–6 on the site of the Deanery of Sint-Donaaskerk *(see below)*. It became the seat of the Bishop of Bruges in 1559 and eventually passed to the provincial governor. It now houses West Flanders Province's press and public relations department.

Romanesque **Sint-Donaaskerk** (St Donatian's Church), the city's earliest known religious foundation, begun around 940, became a cathedral in 1562 and was largely destroyed between 1799 and 1802 by anti-clerical supporters of the French Revolution. You can occasionally visit remains of the excavated choir gallery in the cellars of the **Crowne Plaza Brugge Burg Hotel**. A miniature stone replica of the vanished cathedral stands on the square, along with a plaque recording the murder there of Count Charles the Good in 1127 'because he took the part of the poor.' Among the nearby plane trees, look out for a romantic modern sculpture, *The Lovers,* representing the starry-eyed couples who get married at the Town Hall opposite. You can make a brief detour into adjacent Hoogstraat, to the crumbling (but under restoration) 14th-century **Huis van de Zeven Torens** (House of the Seven Towers) at No 7, though its seven towers have all gone.

Right: symbol of justice atop the Civic Registry

The Liberty of Bruges

Back in the Burg, visit the **Landhuis van het Brugse Vrije** (Palace of the Liberty of Bruges). The 'Liberty' was a district around the city that was important enough to be represented from 1127 alongside Bruges, Ghent and Ypres at the Flemish Estates (a kind of early Parliament). When, in the late 14th-century, the dukes of Burgundy vacated their 11th-century wooden residence on the Burg and decamped across town to the Prinsenhof *(see Itinerary 8, page 48)*, the Liberty's aldermen moved in. Further construction in the 15th century extended the complex south towards Groenerei. In 1520–25, the crumbling residence was rebuilt as the Palace of the Liberty, and most of it was rebuilt again in neoclassical style in 1722–7.

Revolutionary France abolished the Liberty of Bruges during its occupation of the city in 1794 and the palace later became the city's Law Court.

In 1988 it took on a new lease of life as Bruges Council's administrative offices. The tourist office, a historical gem in its own right, is here.

Meeting of Like Minds

The Liberty's burgomasters and aldermen met in the **Renaissancezaal Brugse Vrije** (Renaissance Hall of the Liberty of Bruges; tel: 050-448711; daily 9.30am–5pm), which has been restored to its original condition, with the aldermen's benches in position and the velvet-covered table of the office-holders topped by big brass inkwells and law books. The black Dinant marble fireplace has a superb, carved oak chimneypiece from 1528–9 by Lanceloot Blondeel, celebrating Emperor Charles V's victory in 1525 at Pavia over Francis I of France. Charles, in full armour, with raised sceptre and the orb of empire in his hands – and sporting an impressive codpiece – stands in the centre beneath the double-headed Habsburg eagle, flanked by his grandparents Emperor Maximilian of Austria, Duchess Mary of Burgundy, Ferdinand II of Aragon and Isabela I of Castile, and two medallions of his parents, the engagingly named Philip the Fair and Joanna the Mad. The panels of an alabaster frieze depict the Old Testament story of Suzanna being falsely accused by the Elders, who are then stoned to death – no doubt a salutary tale to the lawmakers who congregated here. The brass handholds hanging from the mantelpiece were for dignitaries to steady themselves while they dried their wet boots at the fire.

The Flemish Renaissance **Burgerlijke Griffie** (Civic Registry) next door, dating from 1534–7, has the city's oldest surviving Renaissance facade, though with Gothic elements, which has been restored to bring out the original colours. Its three scrolled gables are particularly fine. Built as the Town Clerk's office and later used by the court recorder, it now houses the Municipal Archives.

Above: committing the Town Hall to canvas. **Above Right:** the Town Hall's ornate interior
Right: the Palace of the Liberty of Bruges now serves as administrative offices

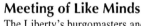

Across Blinde Ezelstraat (to which we will return shortly), the graceful, triple-turreted, Gothic **Stadhuis** (Town Hall), a refined late 14th-century building, is Belgium's oldest town hall. Its magnificent **Gotische Zaal** (Gothic Hall; tel: 050-448711; Tues–Sun 10am–5pm) on the first floor is worth visiting to see its carved-oak vaulted ceiling and biblical murals from 1385–1402, as well as a number of other 19th-century murals relating the city's history. You can also see Marcus Gerard's engraved 1562 *Map of Bruges*.

Renovated in the 1980s, the Town Hall has a pristine look that extends to the statues of biblical and historical figures in the niches on its facade; these replaced the originals, painted by Jan van Eyck and smashed in the 1790s by supporters of Revolutionary France. The facade also bears the coats of arms of the Flemish communes.

The Holy Blood

Continuing clockwise around the square, you come next to the **Heilig-Bloedbasiliek** (Basilica of the Holy Blood; Apr–Sept: daily 9.30am–noon and 2–6pm; Oct–Mar: 10am–noon and 2–4pm, closed Wed pm). On the ground floor is the Romanesque **Sint-Basiliuskapel** (St Basil's Chapel), built in 1134–57 as the church of the now vanished Castle of the Counts, which has a tympanum featuring a bas-relief of the baptism of Christ. The upper floor, reached by a spiral staircase, was remodelled in Gothic style during the 15th century and houses a venerated Relic of the Holy Blood, a scrap of cloth stained with what is said to be blood of Christ, washed from his body

after the Crucifixion by Joseph of Arimathea. It is kept inside a rock-crystal phial, and is reputed to have been brought to Bruges from Jerusalem in 1149 by Count Thierry of Alsace, who received it as a reward for feats of bravery during the Second Crusade. The phial is frequently on display – held in the hands of a church official – and it is often possible to take a close look at it; many people take such an opportunity to kiss the relic.

Also in the church is the **Museum of the Holy Blood,** housing two magnificent gold and silver reliquaries in which the phial is kept when it is not on public display, as well as other interesting items, including two triptych panels (*circa* 1556) by Peter Pourbus depicting the Confraternity of the Holy Blood.

If all this history has left you in need of some light refreshment, relief is at hand in a row of gabled houses beside the basilica, where you will find **Brasserie Tom Pouce,** good for a simple snack rather than anything more adventurous.

Along the Waterside

Afterwards, return to the previously mentioned Blinde Ezelstraat (Blind Donkey Street), a narrow lane that begins with a vaulted arcade between the Town Hall and the Civic Registry. This brings you to a bridge over the canal to Steenhouwersdijk. On your right is a jetty for canal-boat tours.

Cross the bridge and turn right along Groenerei to Huidenvettersplein, where the Tanners' guildhouse, the **Ambachtshuis der Huidenvetters** from 1630–31, is now an exclusive restaurant. In summer, tourists tan their own hides on the magical little square's cafe terraces and street artists record the scene for posterity. Note the column in the middle topped by a pair of lions. It might be a good idea to check out the classic restaurant **Duc de Bourgogne** at No 12 for possible later reference; **'t Mozarthuys** at No 1

is another good bet. At the end of the square, turn briefly left to reach 7 Braambergstraat for a look (or more) at **De Kogge**, an antique tavern in the former Fish Porters' guildhouse from 1637. Retrace your steps and emerge onto **Rozenhoedkaai** (Rosary Quay), which offers the loveliest view of Bruges – canal, waterside houses and Belfry. To your right is another jetty for canal-boat tours. You can take a break here at **'t Klein Venetië** (Little Venice) café, which has a waterside terrace.

Go back through Huidenvettersplein to the classical, colonnaded **Vismarkt** (Fish Market) from 1820–21, one of few notable structures bequeathed by the period of Dutch rule. From Tuesday to Saturday, between 8am and 1pm, you can buy fresh North Sea fish and prawns, or sample the raw herring and cooked prawns prepared at the market. For a more substantial seafood treat, try the market's **De Visscherie** restaurant *(see Eating Out, page 74)*. At weekends, an outpost of the Dijver's antiques and flea market *(see Shopping, page 71)* moves in.

Continue along the waterside. Across the canal you can see a part of the early 16th-century Palace of the Liberty of Bruges in the Burg that was unaffected by rebuilding in 1722–7. The adjacent baroque mansion, **De Caese**, is part of the palace complex that was bought and restored by Paribas Bank in 1988. Keep going into tree-lined Groenerei, past two old stone bridges, Meebrug and Peerdenbrug, to the end of the quay. **Godshuis De Pelikaan** at Nos 8–12, decorated with a relief of a pelican feeding its young (a symbol of Christ), used to be an almshouse and hospital for the poor. It was built in 1634.

Tribute to Jacques Brel

Groenerei curves round into Coupure on a narrow canalside parapet. Keep going to a scenic outlook at Predikheren Bridge. Midway along the canal, Coupure Bridge is favoured by local fishermen and in good weather you can expect to see fishing lines deployed hopefully in the water. Yachts and cabin cruisers are moored along the quay. Make a brief diversion across the bridge to the sensuous sculpture *Marieke* on a triangle

of grass opposite, representing the girl in the great Belgian singer Jacques Brel's song *Ai Marieke*. Adjacent **Bistro De Schaar** at 2 Hooistraat is a good place for a break.

Back on Coupure, then Boninvest, you come next to **Gentpoort** (Ghent Gate), an impressive-looking lump of medieval brickwork from the old city walls built in two phases, 1361–3 and 1401–6.

Turn right here on Gentpoortstraat to neo-Gothic **Heilige-Magdalenakerk** (Blessed Mary Magdalene Church), built 1851–3. Behind the church is 19th-century **Koningin Astridpark** (Queen Astrid Park), one of the city's largest, created by the demise of a Franciscan Abbey. You rarely find tourists here and can admire in peace its blue-and-gold-painted, wrought-iron bandstand from 1859 and central pond with swans.

Above Left: Museum of the Holy Blood reliquary. **Left:** Brasserie Tom Pouce
Above: the bandstand in Queen Astrid Park – a tranquil spot for contemplation

4. LACE, WINDMILLS, ARCHERS AND BEER
(see map, p20–21)

This four- to six-hour itinerary starts with a slew of historic churches, moves eastwards to some of the city's most interesting museums, and ends up at a place where liquid refreshment complements the preceding cultural experience.

To the start: Take De Lijn city buses 1, 3, 4, 6, 8, 11, 13 or 16 to the Markt, then walk a short distance east to Philipstockstraat and Keersstraat.

Sint-Pieterskapel (St Peter's Chapel) in Keersstraat was for centuries the Candlemakers Guild chapel. Demolished in the 18th century, then rebuilt, it is now shared by the United Protestant Church and the Anglican Church. Circle round into Cordoeaniersstraat, pausing for a peek at No 5, the **Brugs Diamanthuis**, in a beautifully restored building dating from 1518 with stepped gable and now a shop with a sparkling display of diamonds.

Now take Sint-Jansplein, Sint-Jansstraat and Korte Riddersstraat to Sint-Maartensplein and **Sint-Walburgakerk** (St Walburga's Church), a magnificent baroque church dating from 1619–43. You should definitely take a look inside, as the former Jesuit church is one of few baroque monuments in this relentlessly Gothic city, sporting an elegant sufficiency of marble and a notable altar, pulpit and communion bench.

Outside again, take Hoornstraat to Verversdijk, where a plaque on the first canalside building to your right informs you that the local poet-priest Guido Gezelle lived here between 1867 and 1872. Continue to the bridge and cross to Sint-Annarei. A brief diversion to the left takes in a restored baroque house at No 22 and a rococo merchant's house at No 27. You would be

well rewarded by keeping the diversion going a little longer and turning right at the end of Sint-Annarei into Blekersstraat, to reach the city's oldest tavern, **Café Vlissinghe** (dating from 1515) at No 2, which has period furniture and a garden terrace. On the way you get a fine view of the junction of two canals.

Churches and Lace

All these diversions are off the main itinerary and if you prefer to skip them, go instead from Sint-Annarei into Sint-Annakerkstraat and Sint-Annaplein to **Sint-Annakerk** (St Anne's Church), built in 1624. Not much for exterior looks, St Anne's compensates with lavish marble baroque decoration that offsets the interior's rather severe lines. Still, it's on a human scale and you get

Left: the baroque St Walburga's Church
Right (top and bottom): at the Lace Centre

the impression it was done to provide comfort for genuine worshippers, rather than as some overstated monument to heavenly glory.

Turn right outside the church on Jeruzalemstraat to Peperstraat and the striking **Jeruzalemkerk** (Jerusalem Church). It was largely built in 1471–83, around a slightly earlier chapel and was the church of the Genoese merchant Adornes family, long resident in Bruges. Pieter Adornes and his brother Jacob, back from a pilgrimage to the Holy Land, set about re-creating Jerusalem's Church of the Holy Sepulchre, down to a replica Tomb of Christ complete with plaster statue. Pieter's son Anselm, a humanist and intellectual who completed the church, was murdered in 1483 while on a diplomatic mission to Scotland for the Duke of Burgundy. His heart alone made the return journey to rest in the church beside his wife Margaretha's more complete remains. Their fine black marble sarcophagus is surmounted by recumbent figures of the couple. Many other family members are buried here. Also notable are the stained-glass windows from 1560 showing prominent Adornes, including Pieter and his wife Elisabeth at prayer.

You now leave churches behind and walk a few steps to the adjacent **Kantcentrum** (Lace Centre; tel: 050-330072; Mon–Fri 10am–noon and 2–6pm, Sat 10am–noon and 2–5pm), in the 15th-century **Jerusalem Almshouse** founded by the Adornes family. The museum has notable antique lace pieces, and in the afternoon you can watch demonstrations of this painstaking craft at a workshop in the former Adornes mansion. At the museum shop you can buy all the materials you need to have a go yourself. Turn into Balstraat, where next door at No 14, lace-making skills are passed on to a new generation at the **Kantschool** (Lace School).

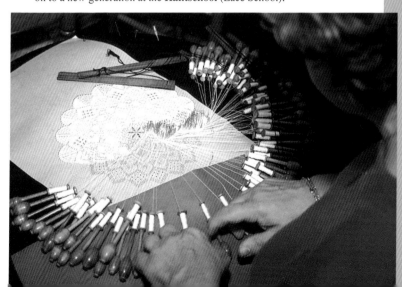

Archers' Guilds and Folk Life

Keep going along Balstraat, passing rooms of the **Stedelijk Museum voor Volkskunde** (Municipal Folklore Museum; tel: 050-448711; Tues–Sun 9.30am–5pm) in the whitewashed cottages of the old Shoemakers Guild almshouse, and at its end turn left into Rolweg where you find the museum entrance. This attractively simple place uses mannequins to depict life in Bruges in times past. Dioramas include a primary school class led by a young priest, a cooper's workshop, spice shop, pipe room, milliner's workshop, confectionery shop, household scenes and an inn, In De Zwarte Kat (The Black Cat) that has real beer on tap. In summer you can play traditional children's games in the garden.

Cross Rolweg, go through Korte Speelmansstraat and turn right on Carmersstraat, passing on the corner a wall-mounted carved wooden shrine from 1760 showing a crucifixion scene and a Madonna and Child statue in a glass case. Keep going past the **Engels Klooster** (English Convent), founded by English nuns in 1629, with a domed church that dates from 1736–9. The poet-priest Guido Gezelle died here; his last words, carved on the facade, translate as: '…and I was so happy to hear the birds sing'.

Further up Carmersstraat, on the other side of the street, is the **Schuttersgilde Sint-Sebastiaan** (St Sebastian Archers Guild; tel: 050-331626; Tues–Thur, Sat 2–5pm). This was a wealthy and influential guild of archers – their patron saint, a 3rd-century Christian martyr, had survived being shot with arrows only to be beaten to death – a status reflected in their sumptuous 16th- to 17th-century headquarters. Among illustrious members were Britain's King Charles II, who paid for the banqueting hall, and his brother Henry, both in exile at the time (a portrait of Henry hangs over the fireplace). Belgian royalty have also been enrolled. Inside, you can see a fine collection of arms and accoutrements, furnishings, gold and silver plate, paintings and other works of art.

Above: the Municipal Folklore Museum in the cottages of the old Shoemakers Guild almshouse

At the end of the street, the **Taverne De Verloren Hoek** at No 178 serves meals and drinks, and is no doubt a welcome place for a mid-point break. You have arrived at Kruisvest and a narrow park that runs beside the ring canal along the line of the long since demolished city walls. To your right stands the **Sint-Janshuismolen** (St John's Mill; Apr–Sept: Tues–Sun 9.30am–12.30pm and 1.30–5pm), a venerable structure used here from 1770 to 1914. This only authentic surviving Bruges windmill was restored in 1964 and operates in the summer as a working museum, with a miller to show you round. A little way north is the **Nieuwe Papegaai Mill**, an oil-mill from Beveren-IJzer in West Flanders that was rebuilt here in 1970, but is no longer in use.

Facing the Sint-Janshuismolen, at 64 Rolweg, the **Guido Gezelle Museum** (tel: 050-448711; Tues–Sun 9.30am–12.30pm and 1.30–5pm) occupies the birthplace of the Flemish poet-priest (1830–99). Surrounded by a large garden, the rather gloomy brick house is interesting enough in itself and contains a variety of objects related to Gezelle's life and work, including copies of his manuscripts and editions of his writing, as well as period furnishings.

Return to Kruisvest, and turn right past a garden called the **Guido Gezelle Warande**, then go right on Stijn Streuvelsstraat to the **Schuttersgilde Sint-Joris** (St George's Archers Guild; tel: 050-335408; open by request only) at No 59. St George's members were crossbowmen and their ornate guild-house contains a fine collection of crossbows. The garden has a vertical target-mast and walkways protected from descending arrows.

Bruges Beer – Past and Present

Back on Kruisvest, there's the **Bonne Chière** wooden stilt-mill, built in 1888 at Olsene in East Flanders and moved to its present location in 1911, though no longer in use. Keep going to **Kruispoort** (Holy Cross Gate), a castle-like fortified gate with drawbridge, one of four remaining fortified gates of the city walls, built in 1366–8 and substantially rebuilt in 1401–6.

You now head away from the ring canal on Langestraat, before turning right on Kerseboomstraat then left to 10 Verbrand Nieuwland and the **Brugs Brouwerij- en Mouterijmuseum** (Bruges Brewing and Malting Museum; tel: 050-330699; Apr–Sept: Wed–Sun 2–6pm), in an old malthouse. The museum holds beer vats, brewing equipment and other mementos of its parent brewery *(see below)* and the 31 breweries operating in the city at the turn of the 19th century, including a period cafe.

Round the corner at 45 Langestraat, there's more for beer lovers at the **Brouwerij De Gouden Boom** (De Gouden Boom Brewery; tel: 050-330699; guided visits for groups by request only; reserve two weeks in advance), which has been operating since 1587. You can watch local brews such as Brugse Tarwebier, Brugse Tripel and Abdij Steenbrugge being produced, and taste the finished product.

Right: St John's Mill

city itineraries

5. THE MERCHANTS' QUARTER *(see map, p20–21)*

This two-hour itinerary covers the trading places of the old mercantile district north of the Markt.

To the start: Take De Lijn city buses 1, 3, 4, 6, 8, 11, 13 or 16 to the Markt, then walk a short distance north to Vlamingstraat.

Going north on Vlamingstraat, you cross Kraanplein, named after a municipal crane used for loading and unloading barges on the canal here – but both crane and canal have vanished. On the left at No 29, the neoclassical **Koninklijke Stadsschouwburg** (Royal Municipal Theatre) dating from 1869, with colonnaded upper facade, was the city's main venue for opera, classical

music, theatre and dance until the Concertgebouw opened in 2002. A sculpture in front represents Papageno from Mozart's opera *The Magic Flute*.

A few doors along at No 33, the sandstone **Genuese Loge** (Genoese Lodge) from 1399 was the trading house of Genoese merchants in the city until they left in 1516 and is the best preserved of the surviving trading houses of foreign merchants. Used for a few subsequent centuries as a cloth exchange, the Saaihalle, it was restored in 1983 and is now a cultural centre. Look on the arch above the doorway for a relief of St George slaying the Dragon. The bell-gable is from 1720.

Fascinating Facades

Across narrow Grauwwerkersstraat (while you are passing, you might like to check out an original 13th-century facade at Nos 2–4), the **Huis Ter Beurze** from 1453 at No 35 is of great historical interest. As a bank and the residence of the Van der Beurze family, it was frequented by foreign merchants and bankers. The area became known as Beurzplaats and was the city's financial centre until the 16th century – from it comes the word *bourse* for a stock exchange. Appropriately, the house is now a branch of KBC Bank.

Cross Vlamingstraat to Academiestraat and the **National House of Florence**, built in 1430 but greatly altered over the centuries (it now houses the ultra-smart restaurant De Florentijnen). Florentine merchants had their base here. On the facade is a plaque quoting a passage from Dante's *The Divine Comedy* that refers to Bruges.

A short way along Academiestraat at Nos 14–18, prominent merchants and bankers used to meet in the late-Gothic **Poortersloge** (Burghers' Lodge). The ornate 15th-century building, with a high bell tower, was headquarters of an exclusive local society, De Witte Beer (The White Bear), which among other things organised jousting tournaments. Look in a niche at the end for a statue from 1417 of a bear carrying a shield with masonic symbols, a badge of the city. Restored in the early 1900s after a period as the City Academy, it now houses the Bruges National Archive.

Above: detail at the Huis Ter Beurze, which dates back to 1453

Adjacent Spanjaardstraat was the centre of the city's Spanish merchants in the 16th and 17th centuries, and many fine mansions in this area testify to their wealth. Among the finest, the **De la Torre House** at No 16 (now a clinic) has an ornate Renaissance portal. Ignatius de Loyola, the Spanish priest who founded the Jesuits, was a frequent guest in the house at No 9 between 1528 and 1530.

Artists' Statues

Back on Academiestraat, walk a few paces into Jan van Eyckplein, where at No 2 the sandstone, late-Gothic **Oud Tolhuis** (Old Toll House) from 1477–8 was where taxes were levied on goods brought into the city by boat. It now houses West Flanders Province's archives and information centre. Note the heraldic device above the entrance inscribed with insignia of the Order of the Golden Fleece, founded in Bruges in 1430. Cross the square for a close-up view of a **statue of Jan van Eyck**, the Flemish artist who lived in Bruges from 1425 until his death in 1441.

Re-cross the square and turn into Woensdagmarkt in which is a statue from 1871 of the German-born artist and resident of Bruges, Hans Memling, looking rather downhearted. Pass through neighbouring Oosterlingenplein to Krom Genthof. The **Oosterlingenhuis** (House of the Easterners) at No 1 was the local headquarters of the Baltic Hanseatic League, which was trading with Bruges as early as the 13th century. It was built in 1478–81, but only part survives in what is now the Hotel Bryghia. Round the corner in Genthof, a privately owned 15th-century house at No 7 is one of the city's two surviving buildings with timber facades. From here you can easily jump to the start of Itinerary 6, and because this has been a brief excursion there should be plenty of time to do so.

Above: Burgher's Lodge, Jan van Eyckplein
Right: the sign of the stocking-maker

6. CANALSIDE BRUGES *(see map, p20–21)*

The reward of this four-hour itinerary is that you escape from the city centre and its touristic obsessions, to a long, graceful canal that leads to the northern edge of the old city.

To the start: Take De Lijn city buses 4 or 8 to Gouden Handstraat at Langerei, then cross the canal bridge to Sint-Annarei.

You may find it hard to believe that this tranquil, house-lined waterway would once have been filled with canal barges. Continue into Potterierei, where at No 15 is the only place that really warrants a break on this itinerary: **Koto**, in the De Medici Hotel, is an upmarket Japanese restaurant that is definitely not for the budget-conscious. At No 72, pass through a wooden gateway to the former Cistercian **Ter Duinen Abdij** (Abbey of the Dunes) from 1627, formerly cstablished at Koksijde on the North Sea coast but whose monks were forced out by encroaching seas in 1560. Since 1833 this has been an Episcopal seminary. You can visit its 18th-century church, gardens and greenhouse with permission, obtainable at the main entrance.

Further along, **Onze-Lieve-Vrouw van de Potterie** (Our Lady of the Pottery) is a hospice that was founded in 1276 and expanded from the 14th to the 17th centuries. Most of the complex is now a home for senior citizens. A section, including the hospital ward from 1529 and the 14th- to 15th-century cloisters, serves as the **Potterie Museum** (tel: 050-448711; Tues–Sun 9.30am–12.30pm and 1.30–5pm), displaying a rich collection of tapestries, 15th- to 17th-century furniture, silverware, religious objects and books, and 16th- and 17th-century Flemish paintings.

The adjoining hospice chapel from 1329 was the chapel of the Potters Guild. A second church, from 1623, has a fine baroque interior containing a statue from around 1300 of Our Lady of the Pottery that is said to have miraculous powers, and a 16th-century tapestry of the Nativity.

Continue to the end of Potterierei, then turn south a short distance to

reach the **Koeleweimolen** (Tues–Sun 9.30am–12.30pm and 1.30–5pm), dating from 1765. One of a quartet of windmills in the ring canal park *(see Itinerary 4, page 41, for the other three)*, it was in use at Meulebeke in West Flanders before being rebuilt here in 1996.

The Harbour and Beyond

Going north again brings you to **Dampoort**, part of the old harbour that is still busy with barges sailing to and from Zeebrugge. Beyond, on the road to Damme *(see Excursion 1, page 53)*, is a jetty on Noorweegse Kaai from where the stern-wheel paddle steamer *De Lamme Goedzaak* sails along the Bruges–Sluis Canal to Damme. In Komvest beside the harbour are the Art Deco offices from 1925 of a demolished factory that now house the Dutch Consulate.

Head south on Langerei, past the **Duinenbrug** drawbridge, and past the dilapidated Sareptha at Nos 25–6. Formerly a convent of Augustinian Canonesses, who moved here in 1617 and were evicted in 1784 by Emperor Joseph II, it is now an educational institution. A little further, at No 7, the 18th-century offices of the charitable institution **Berg van Caritate** (Mount of Charity) now, ironically, houses the local office of the Ministry of Finance.

Turn right into Sint-Gilliskoorstraat, to **Sint-Gilliskerk** (St Giles's Church). Begun around 1241 in cruciform early-Gothic style, it was drastically altered in the 15th century, giving it three aisles. Among treasures you can see inside are a superb organ and a cycle of four paintings from 1774 by Jan Garemijn depicting the history of the Trinitarian Brothers. The painter Hans Memling was buried in the churchyard in 1494.

Come out into Sint-Gilliskerkstraat, and by way of Gouden-Handstraat and Oost Gistelhof return to the waterside at Augusteinenrei, beside the stone benches of the 13th-century **Augustijnenbrug** (Augustinian Bridge), and cross over. Stroll to the left if you like along handsome canalside Spaanse Loskaai and Groene Handrei. Otherwise turn right into Kortewinkel, pausing, if the big wooden door at No 10 is open, for a look at the pretty courtyard garden of the Jezuiten Huis. Adjacent to No 2 is one of two surviving – though barely – timber facades in Bruges. You come now to Vlamingstraat, where No 100 is an early 16th-century house built for goldsmith Herman van Houtvelde – you get a fine view of its crumbling rear from Vlamingbrug.

The neo-Gothic **Heilige Hartkerk** (Sacred Heart Church), which was built in 1879–85, used to belong to the Jesuits, but Celebrations Entertainment (tel: 050-347572) now use it for their 'Bryggia My Love' multimedia trip through Bruges history (Apr–Oct: every hour 10am–5pm) and 'Brugge Anno 1468' medieval banquet and show (Apr–Oct: Thur–Sat 7.30–10pm; Nov–Mar: Sat 7.30–10pm).

Left: canal view from Potterie
Above: taking to the waters

7. TO THE RING CANAL *(see map, p18–19)*

Stroll through a shopping and religious quarter west of the Markt on this four-hour itinerary, which passes through a busy market square.

To the start: Take De Lijn city buses 1, 3, 4, 6, 8, 11, 13 or 16 to the Markt, then walk to Oude Burg at the rear of the Hallen.

Off Oude Burg, turn left into Karthuizerinnenstraat for a look at the 16th- to 17th-century **Karthuizerinnen Klooster** (Carthusian Convent), now social services offices. The convent church at No 2 is a military chapel; its crypt holds ashes of Dachau concentration camp victims and on the walls are plaques bearing the names of the dead from both world wars.

Return to Oude Burg, to the **Hof van Watervliet** at No 27, built around 1450 for the patrician Jan de Baenst, whose loyalty to the House of Burgundy earned him both wealth and the enmity of his fellow citizens. The mansion was then home to Pieter Lanchals, Crown Prince Maximilian's pro-taxation *consigliere*, executed by unenthusiastic taxpayers in 1488 – ironically the house now accommodates the Hof Lanchals health and welfare centre.

This brings you to **Simon Stevinplein** and its bronze sculpture of Simon Stevin (1548–1620), a Bruges mathematician and scientist who thought up the decimal system and the science of hydrostatics, and who fled to Holland from Spanish anti-Protestant persecution around 1580. The excellent **Bhavani** restaurant at No 5 should appeal to devotees of Indian cuisine.

The Cathedral and its Museum

Continue along Oude Burg to richly decorated **Sint-Salvatorskathedraal** (Holy Saviour's Cathedral; Mon 2–5.45pm, Tues–Fri 9am–noon and 2–5.45pm, Sat 9am–noon and 2–3.30pm, Sun 9–10.15am and 2–5.45pm). The city's oldest parish church dates from the 9th century. Now mainly 12th- to 15th-century Gothic, with neo-Romanesque elements, it has a 100m (325ft) brick belfry. Holy Saviour's was upgraded to a cathedral in 1834 as a replacement for demolished St Donatian's *(see Itinerary 3, page 33)*. On its 15th-century wooden choir stalls are the coats of arms of the

Knights of the Golden Fleece. Other notable features are a baroque rood-screen surmounted by the sculpture *God the Father* (1682) by Artus Quellin the Younger, an elaborate pulpit, and Gobelins tapestries beside the altar.

The **Cathedral Museum** (Sun–Fri 2–5pm) houses among other items an early 16th-century portrait of Charles V attributed to Jan van Orley, and the Cathedral Treasury of gold and silver religious vessels, reliquaries and episcopal vestments. Emerge into Sint-Salvatorskerkhof, and sidestep briefly into Heilige-Geeststraat, to pass a neoclassical mansion from 1740 at No 4 that is now the **Episcopal Palace**.

Left: Oude Burg seen from Simon Stevinplein

city itineraries

Around 't Zand

Sint-Salvatorskerkhof runs into Korte Vuldersstraat, then Zuidzandstraat, which enters the east side of **'t Zand**, a big, open square lined with cafes, shops and restaurants. Vrijdagmarkt, along its western face, has a Saturday morning street market. A large modern sculpture group in four parts around an ornamental fountain in the centre of 't Zand features diverse images of Flanders. *Bathing Women* represents Bruges, Antwerp, Ghent and Kortrijk; *Landscape in Flanders* the polders; *The Fishermen* recalls the city's links with the North Sea; and *The Cyclists* illustrates a popular local pastime. At the south end of the square is Bruges's shiny new **Concertgebouw** concert and opera hall, built to accompany the city's stint as one of the European Capitals of Culture in 2002.

Leave 't Zand by its southwestern corner, into Boeveriestraat. At the top, on the left, a cluster of almshouses – the **Van Campen** (1636), **Van Peenen** (1629), **Gloribus** (1634) and **Sucx** (1649) – spreads into neighbouring side streets. A little further, on the right, is the **Capucijnerabdij** (Capuchin Abbey), from 1869. Beyond this, across the street again, is the brick-built Benedictine cloister of **Sint-Godelieve Abdij** (St Godelieve Abbey), whose nuns established themselves here in 1623.

You now pass the **Dumery Bell** (from the Belfry in the Markt), now framed and set down on the pavement, recalling the vanished 18th-century bell-foundry of Joris Dumery. After this comes **Godshuis de Moor** (De Moor Almshouse) at Nos 52–76, founded in 1480 by Donaas de Moor, who had to flee the town in 1488 for backing the unpopular Maximilian of Austria.

At the end of Boeveriestraat, turn north through the pleasant ring canal park as far as the medieval **Nieuw Waterhuis** (New Water House), which drew water from the canal using a horse-powered waterwheel.

Above: *Bathing Women*, representing Bruges, Antwerp, Ghent and Kortrijk
Right: interior detail, Holy Saviour's Cathedral, which dates to the 9th century

8. PRINCELY BRUGES *(see map, p18–19)*

The highlight of this two- to three-hour itinerary through a busy shopping district to the ring canal is an ancient royal palace, the Prinsenhof – though, sadly, a considerable amount of imagination is required to picture its former glory.

To the start: Take De Lijn city buses 1, 3, 4, 6, 8, 11, 13 or 16 to the Markt, then walk a short distance west on Geldmuntstraat to Muntplein.

On the way, mouth-watering cakes and other sweet things in the window of **De Medici Sorbetière** on Geldmuntstraat more or less demand attention. In Muntplein, the small, bronze equestrian statue from 1901, called *Flandria Nostra (Our Flanders)* is of Mary of Burgundy, who died in 1482 at the age of 25 after a fall from her horse while hunting in the forest. She now resides in a fine mausoleum in the Church of Our Lady *(see Itinerary 2, page 29)*. In the circumstances an equestrian pose doesn't seem entirely fitting, but she is nevertheless depicted riding side-saddle, looking for all the world like an expert. Muntplein and Geldmuntstraat recall the coin mint that once stood in Geerwijnstraat – *munt* means mint and *geld* means money.

Go west on Noordzandstraat and turn right at the next street, Prinsenhof, named for the site of the **Prinsenhof** (Prince's Court). This royal residence of the houses of Burgundy and Habsburg was built, around an earlier structure, by Duke Philip the Good in time for his marriage in 1430 to Isabelle of Portugal. Not much survives of the palace and you see clearly the signs of repairs and additions as you walk through the ornamental gate, yet the Prinsenhof is still imposing. The cash-strapped Habsburgs sold it in 1662 to the nuns of St Francis, who in 1794 shipped out ahead of the incoming Revolutionary, anti-clerical French. The property was sold again, and municipal housing was built on its extensive grounds. In 1888, nuns, this time the sisters of the French Dames de la Retraite, were back, but a century later a private concern bought the building, and it is now used for exhibitions, conferences and concerts.

Above: temptations in Geldmuntstraat
Left: get your ice creams here

Off the Tourist Trail

From this point on, none of the attractions are exactly unmissable, but the walk gives you a fascinating glimpse of life in Bruges away from the tourist-orientated city-centre attractions. Continue around into Ontvangersstraat, then turn left into Moerstraat, and across the canal into Beenhouwersstraat, to **Hof Sebrechts**, a park that replaced the demolished St Elisabeth's Convent. In summer, the park is transformed into an open-air gallery for modern sculpture. Come out into Moerstraat, and go right to handsome Speelmansrei, on the corner of which stands the little **Speelmanskapel** (Minstrel's Church) from 1421, the chapel of the Guild of Minstrels, now owned by a private foundation.

At the end of Speelmansrei, which runs alongside the canal, turn right and walk along Smedenstraat for four blocks – maybe stopping for a break at **Passeviet**, a fine traditional bistro at No 48, which has a pavement terrace. Suitably refreshed, turn right into Kreupelenstraat, to the church of **Onze-Lieve-Vrouw van Blindekens** (Our Lady of the Blind), a bright, plain 17th-century church with a carved pulpit from 1659 and a 14th-century gilded silver statue of the *Madonna and Child* above a side altar. On 15 August each year, to celebrate the feast of the Assumption, a procession winds from here to Onze-Lieve-Vrouw van de Potterie (Our Lady of the Pottery) church in the northeast of the city *(see Itinerary 6, page 44)*. Around the church, connected by an alleyway between Kreupelenstraat and Kammakerssstraat, is a cluster of old almshouses, the **Van Pamel**, **Marius Voet** and **Laurentia Soutieu**.

Continue along Smedenstraat to the **Smedenpoort** (Marshal's Gate), which dates from 1367–8 with 17th-century additions. This is one of the four surviving fortified gates of the nine that were once dotted round the now vanished medieval city walls.

9. THE DONKEY QUARTER *(see map, p20–21)*

This two- to three-hour itinerary takes in historic patrician houses on the way to the ring canal and a fortified city gate. It ends at a church enriched by patrician patronage.

To the start: Take De Lijn city buses 1, 2, 3, 4, 5, 6, 7, 8, 9, 13, 15, 16, 17 or 25, to Biekorf, then walk the short distance to Eiermarkt.

A rococo stone fountain from 1761 stands in bustling Eiermarkt, which is lined with modest restaurants and cafes. Go north on Sint-Jakobstraat, passing the 1890s Art Nouveau facade of bistro-restaurant **Pietje Pek** at No 13. Continue to the neoclassical **Stedelijk Conservatorium** (Municipal Conservatory) at Nos 23–5, which you can enter – if you

Right: bistro with 1890s Art Nouveau facade

have the confidence to pretend you're a student or a maestro – and swing right through a waiting room to admire the restored stone buildings around an inner courtyard.

The route then brings you to the 16th-century **Boterhuis** (Butter House) at No 38, a turreted and arched building that was used as a dairy centre from the 17th century. It is now occupied by the De Lumière art cinema, a hotel and an antiques shop.

Passing under the arch, you now enter Naaldenstraat, where the 15th-century **Hof Bladelin** (Bladelin House; closed to the public) was once the home of Pieter Bladelin (1410–72), treasurer to Duke Philip the Good of Burgundy and a patron of Flemish artists, among them Rogier van der Weyden. Take a moment to look for the neo-Gothic niche (1892) on the outside showing Bladelin kneeling before a crowned Madonna and Child. The Medici Bank of Florence took over the house in 1466 and ordered a remodelling that included the provision of a courtyard and ornamental garden, thought to be the earliest Renaissance work in the Low Countries. Two medallions from 1469 on the courtyard facade depict Lorenzo (the Magnificent) de Medici and his wife Clarisse Orsini.

Along Ezelstraat

Continue to Grauwwerkersstraat and cross the canal on **Ezelbrug** (Donkey Bridge) into Ezelstraat, a street lined with undistinguished shops. From adjacent Pottenmakkerstraat there is a view across the water of a short surviving stretch of the 12th-century **city walls**, including a defensive tower that dates from 1127.

You could break off at this point and go straight to St James's Church *(see opposite)*, because none of the other sights could be described as outstanding – on the other hand, now's as good a time as any to see them. For a break, the rustic **Crêperie de Bretoen** at No 4 offers 60 kinds of pancake.

Further along the street, the 15th-century **Karmelietenkerk** (Church of the Carmelite Monastery) has a gloomy baroque interior that dates from 1688–91. Its monks have been here since 1633, and though the French expelled them in 1795, they returned after Napoleon's defeat.

Continue along Ezelstraat to the **Joseph**

Top: sculpture on the facade of Joseph Ryelandt Hall. **Above:** adornment at the Church of the Carmelite Monastery. **Right:** Donkey Gate, once a portal through the 14th-century city

Ryelandtzaal (Joseph Ryelandt Hall). This was once the convent church of the Carmelites, then in the 1820s it became an Anglican church. Since 1983 it has been used as a concert hall, named after the Bruges composer Joseph Ryelandt (1870–1965), and recitals and other performances take place here. A sculpture group from 1987 on the facade represents the *Art of Music*. Further along the street, past the **Orthodox Church of SS Constantine and Helena**, you can take a pleasant stroll in the small but densely planted **Pastoor Van Haecke Plantsoen** (Pastor Van Haecke Garden); you'll find the entrance beside the Green Cross pharmacy sign at No 123.

Donkey Gate and St James's

At the end of Ezelstraat, cross Koningin Elisabethlaan to the **Ezelpoort** (Donkey Gate), also known as Sint-Jacobspoort (St James's Gate), one of four surviving fortified gates of the nine that once allowed passage through the now vanished 14th-century city walls. Built in 1369–70 on the Ostend road, it has been rebuilt several times over the centuries. The moat beside the gate usually has an astonishing number of swans.

Go back along Ezelstraat to Sint-Jakobstraat and turn right past the Krokodil children's toy shop to ponderously Gothic **Sint-Jacobskerk** (St James's Church), built in the 1240s over an earlier chapel and rebuilt in the 15th century, whose true beauty lies within. The church benefited from its position close to the Prinsenhof, an area that attracted the rich and influential who wanted to own houses where they could more easily see and be seen by the monarch – the dukes of Burgundy and foreign merchants and local worthies, such as the wealthy Moreel, Portinari and De Gros families, paid for much of the church's decoration and paintings.

Look particularly in the nave for the *Triptych of the Legend of St Lucy* (1480), the work of an artist known simply as the Master of the Legend of St Lucy. It depicts the saint, martyred around AD 304 in Sicily during the persecution of Diocletian, giving away her worldy goods to the poor and being sentenced to a life of prostitution, to which not even two oxen are strong enough to drag her. There's also an intricately carved wooden pulpit with figures representing the continents at its base.

Excursions

1. DAMME *(see maps, p54 & 56)*

Damme, just 6km (4 miles) from Bruges, is noted for its medieval archi-tecture, traditional Flemish restaurants, and scenic canalside location. Including getting there and back by car or bus, allow at least four hours for this itinerary, longer if you go by bicycle.

To the start: From April to September you can take De Lijn bus 799 from outside Bruges train station (there is no regular bus service the rest of the year) or the stern-wheel paddle steamer Lamme Goedzak, *which sails five times daily between Noorweegse Kaai in the north of Bruges and Damme, a 35-minute cruise along the poplar-lined canal. You can also go there by tour bus, taxi, car, bicycle, and on foot.*

The medieval outer harbour of Bruges, Damme was where merchant ships loaded and unloaded until silting of the Zwin inlet in the Scheldt estuary closed off access to the sea around 1520, bringing to an end the town's pros-perity. Charles the Bold, Duke of Burgundy, and Margaret of York, the sister of England's King Edward IV, were married here in 1468. The village has lately reinvented itself as the Flemish 'village of books', modelled on Britain's Hay-on-Wye, with a dozen bookshops selling second-hand and rare editions.

The Gothic **Stadhuis** (Town Hall), built in the Markt in 1464–8, was paid for with taxes on imported wine and herring. On its facade are statues of, among others, Charles the Bold, Margaret of York, Count Philip of Alsace, and Countess Johanna and Countess Margaret of Constantinople. In front stands a statue of Jacob van Maerlant (1230–96), the 'father of Dutch poetry', who lived in Damme from around 1270 and wrote his most important works here. Adjacent to the Town Hall, the **Pallieter** at 12 Kerkstraat is a relaxed place for a drink and a snack.

Opposite the Town Hall, at 3 Jacob van Maerlantstraat, a 15th-century patrician house called **De Grote Sterre** was, in the 17th cen-tury, the residence of the Spanish governor. It now houses the tourist office and the **Tijl Uilenspiegel Museum** (tel: 050-353319; mid-April–mid-Oct: daily 9am–noon and 2–6pm, from 10am weekends and public hols; rest of year: Mon–Fri 9am–noon and 2–5pm, week-ends and public hols 2–5pm only). Tijl Uilen-spiegel, a 14th-century German folk-tale character, arrived in Damme by a circuitous route and has been adopted by the village.

Further along, at No 13, the 15th-century **Saint-Jean d'Angélly House**, where in 1468

Left: pedal power in Damme
Right: modern bikers, outside the old Town Hall

Charles the Bold married Margaret of York, was the headquarters of French wine traders. Across the road, **De Lieve** restaurant, with a pavement terrace in summer, is the classiest place in town for lunch or dinner. At the corner of Jacob van Maerlantstraat and Ketelstraat you can see the foundations of a lock-gate, the **Sas van de Lieve**, part of the harbour installations of a 13th-century canal connecting Damme with Ghent.

Corneliestraat opposite leads south to **Haringmarkt** (Herring Market), a lawn with an old fountain at one end which is bordered by whitewashed, red-tiled houses with painted wooden shutters. A reputed 28 million Baltic herring were processed here annually during the 15th century. Beside it are some remains of Damme's medieval fortifications.

Take Pottenbakkersstraat, passing cottages and bookshops, to Kerkstraat and turn left. **Sint-Janshospitaal** (St John's Hospital; Apr–Sept: Mon 2–6pm, Tues–Sat 10am–noon and 2–6pm, Sun 11am–noon and 2–6pm; Oct–Mar: Sat–Sun 2–4.30pm) was endowed in 1249 by Margaret of Constantinople as a hospice. The main building is Gothic, but other parts are of a later date. Its museum displays ecclesiastical objects, furniture, paintings, pottery and funerary sculpture.

A Fine View Over Damme

Further along Kerkstraat, **Onze-Lieve-Vrouwekerk** (Our Lady's Church; May–Oct: daily 10am–noon and 2.30–5.30pm) is a squat Gothic edifice from around 1340, built over a chapel from 1225. It proved too big for the village's diminished needs in the straitened economic circumstances from the 16th century onwards, and in 1725 part of it was demolished. Climb the tower for a fine view over Damme and the surrounding polderland.

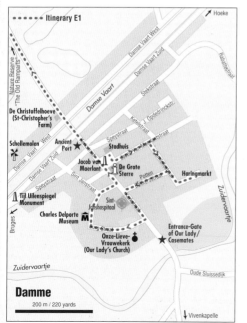

Take Burgstraat, which begins as a tree-lined cobbled path next to the church and curves around the back of St John's Hospital, to the **Charles Delporte Museum** (Easter and July–Aug school holidays; opening times vary, tel: 050-353319), containing paintings and sculptures by this modern Belgian artist.

Go via the Markt to Damse Vaart-Zuid on the Bruges–Sluis Canal, dug by Spanish prisoners of war in 1811–12 as part of Napoleon's scheme to connect Dunkirk and the Scheldt beyond the reach of blockading British warships. A little way along from the jetty where the *Lamme Goedzak* docks, a modern sculp-

Above: a traditional form of footwear
Right: Ghent town centre

ture group illustrates the Tijl Uilenspiegel legend. Cross the canal bridge, pausing to admire the view. Facing you is whitewashed 18th-century **De Christoffelhoeve** (St Christopher's Farm), with a huge barn and ornamental gates. A little further on are the **Old Ramparts** of the town walls, the line of which form a nature reserve.

Back at the canal, a short way along Damse Vaart-West, is the **Schellemolen** (June and Sept: Sat–Sun 2–5.30pm; July–Aug: daily 10.30am–12.30pm and 2–5pm), a windmill built in 1867.

2. GHENT (GENT) *(see maps, p56 & 59)*

This day-long itinerary explores the highlights of a city that is not as pretty as Bruges, but has as many, if not more, stellar sights and a gritty urban reality that gives a more fully developed character.

To the start: There are direct trains at least hourly between Bruges and Gent-Sint-Pieters station, and the journey takes just 20 minutes. Take tram 1, 10, 11 or 12 to Korenmarkt from under the bridge to your left as you exit Ghent station; don't walk into the centre, as the route is long and uninteresting. By road, take the A10 (E40).

The extravagant pile on the west side of Korenmarkt is the neo-Gothic former head post office and telephone office from 1904, now a shopping centre. On the east side, **Sint-Niklaaskerk** (St Nicholas's Church) is the genuine Gothic article, a mix of Tournai and Flemish variations on this theme. The church has been closed for renovation for a long time. In partial compensation, stroll along Klein Turkije at the side of the church for a look at a gloomy 13th-century former inn, **Den Rooden Hoed** at No 4. A wall plaque tells you that Albrecht Dürer lodged here in 1521 when he was court painter to Charles V.

Continue into Gouden Leeuwplein, where you pass a grounded bell, De Triomfante, which was forged in 1659 and was dropped (figuratively speaking) from the Belfry carillon when it cracked in 1914, and a sculpture fountain with five naked, kneeling figures, on the way to the **Belfort en Lakenhalle**

(Belfry and Cloth Hall; Apr–Nov: guided tours daily 10am–4pm). The 14th-century Belfry is 91m (295ft) high. As in Bruges, it was a symbol of the city's civic pride and the place where Ghent's privileges (civic charters) were guarded under multiple locks. In 1659 The 37-bell carillon (concerts every Fri and Sun 11.30am–12.30pm) that resides on the fifth floor was forged using the brass from a single giant bell that had hung in the tower. If you have climbed Bruges' Belfry, you might be glad to learn that this one has a lift. Note the gilded copper dragon at the top. The tourist office is in the Belfry cellar.

Cloth was stored and traded at the 1425–45 Cloth Hall, which also served as a prison. This newer section is nicknamed De Mammelokker (The Suckler) after a relief above the doorway that shows the Roman legend of Cimon, starving to death in prison, being suckled by his daughter Pero.

Across the north end of Gouden Leeuwplein is Botermarkt and the **Stadhuis** (Town Hall; guided tours only, tel: 09-233 0772 to hire a guide), built in two phases, Gothic and Renaissance, from 1518–35 and 1572–1620. Political and financial difficulties meant the work wasn't completely finished until 19th-century neo-Gothic devotees took up the cudgels, or stonemason's hammers. Even with a multiplicity of styles, this is one of Europe's most handsome town halls. Inside, you can visit the magnificent **Pacificatiezaal**, where the

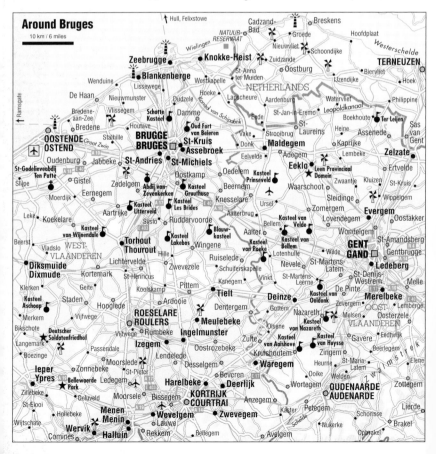

Around Bruges

Pacification of Ghent, aimed (fruitlessly) at ending the religious wars in the Low Countries, was signed in 1576. Across Botermarkt is the **Sint-Jorishof Hotel**, a lodging house since 1228, which counts Mary of Burgundy, Charles V and Napoleon among its illustrious former guests.

Return past the Belfry and Cloth Hall into Sint-Baafsplein, past the neo-Renaissance **Koninklijke Nederlandse Schouwburg** (Royal Netherlandic Theatre) from 1899, to **Sint-Baafskathedraal** (St Bavo's Cathedral). Originally plain Sint-Janskerk (St John's Church), it was promoted to cathedral status in 1561. Built between the 13th and 16th centuries on the site of a 12th-century Romanesque chapel, this is one of the world's great Gothic cathedrals. Inside its vast space are a number of historical treasures, including a painting (*St Bavo*, 1624) by Rubens, a rococo pulpit in marble and oak from 1745, statues and tomb sculptures of various bishops of Ghent, and a set of escutcheons of the Knights of the Golden Fleece.

Van Eyck's Polyptych Altarpiece

What most visitors come to see, though, is Jan van Eyck's polyptych altarpiece of 20 oak panels, *The Adoration of the Mystic Lamb* (*circa* 1432), exhibited in the former baptismal chapel, on the left as you enter the cathedral. The story it tells is that of the Christian mysteries, in particular that of the eucharist. But its use of colour and naturalistic rendering of people and scenery sounded the death-knell for the formal religious art of the Middle Ages. There is an entrance fee to view the polyptych (you can see a ragged copy in miniature free in a chapel off the ambulatory, but it really isn't quite the same).

Take narrow Biezekapelstraat from the corner of Sint-Baafsplein, passing a fine neo-Renaissance house on your left. At the corner where the street doglegs to the right is the city's **Koninklijk Conservatorium** (Royal Conservatory), occupying the 14th- to 15th-century **Achtersikkel** house, a medley of Gothic and Renaissance styles that belonged to the medieval Van der Sikkelen family.

Above: detail from van Eyck's polyptych *The Adoration of the Mystic Lamb*

If, at the end of Biezekapelstraat, you look back, you will catch a fine view of St Bavo's tower framed by the street's houses. The end of the street is itself framed by two more Van der Sikkelen houses.

Cross over to Zandberg, marked, by a water-pump attached to a stone **obelisk** with a perfunctory imperial eagle at the top, an ensemble erected by the French occupation authorities to commemorate Napoleon's visit in 1810. You may well wonder why they bothered. The **De Warempel** fish and vegetarian restaurant at 8 Koningstraat might tempt you to take a break here.

The Friday Market Place

Passing through both Vlas Markt and Sint-Jacobs Vlas Markt, you should arrive at **Sint-Jacobskerk** (St James's Church). You need not bother going inside; it's worthy of mention only as a landmark on your way to **Vrijdagmarkt**. This big, open square hosts the Friday Market that its name implies and generally fills the role of *Grote Markt* that Ghent, unlike most Flemish towns and cities, doesn't have. In the centre of the square is a martial sculpture from 1863 of the wealthy merchant **Jacob van Artevelde** (*circa* 1290–1345), who led Ghent in rebellion against the count of Flanders, on the side of England's Edward III during the Hundred Years War. He was murdered during a riot. His arm is outstretched, as if still hoping to persuade the good burghers that King Ted is their man.

In the northern corner is a building, dating back to 1899, that served as the headquarters of the **Ghent Socialist Workers Society**. The gigantic, gold letters on the facade that proclaim the unity of all the world's workers would have been enough to alarm any passing capitalist. The **Keizershof** restaurant is a fashionable place for dinner, while the **Bier Academie** (also known as Dulle Griet) is a fine Old Flemish tavern with no fewer than 250 beers on

Above: Sint-Michielskerk

offer, among them potent Kwak. You have to deposit a shoe before they will serve you one of these because the special wooden-framed glasses have a tendency to disappear – some may consider it a fair trade.

Leave Vrijdagmarkt on Groot Kanonplein (Big Cannon Square), so called because of the massive cannon that sits in it. Cross the Leie by the bridge at Merseniersstraat to Kraanlei, pausing only to admire the highly decorated old houses at Nos 77 and 79. Behind Kraanlei is the restored **Patershol** district and it's worth taking a stroll through its medieval streets, and maybe calling at the Vier Tafels restaurant at 6 Plotersgracht. Back on Kraanlei is **Het Huis van Alijn** (Alijn House; tel: 09 269 2350; Tues–Sun 11am–5pm), the local folklore museum.

Castle and Medieval Port

At its end, across Geldmuntstraat, is Sint-Veerleplein on which stands the grim **Gravensteen** (Castle of the Counts; tel: 09 269 3730; daily Apr–Sept 9am–6pm; Oct–Mar 9am–5pm), which dates back to 1190. The counts of Flanders' clear message of their military power did not deter the Ghentenaars from insurrection, and though this invariably ended in tears, they came back for more whenever they felt that their rights were being trampled on. Inside, you can visit the dungeons and torture chamber that played such an important part in the counts' hearts-and-minds campaign.

Cross the Lieve canal by the bridge on Rekelingestraat, into Burgstraat. Then, turn left into Jan Breydelstraat, where you will find the **Museum voor Sierkunst en Vormgeving** (Museum of Decorative Arts and Design; tel: 09 267 9999; Tues–Sun 10am–6pm). You pass the excellent **Jan Breydel** French restaurant, where in the summer months you can dine on an outdoor terrace overlooking the meeting point of the River Leie and the Lieve canal.

You come now to **Korenlei**, which together with its across-the-water neighbour **Graslei**, formed the heart of the medieval port. Guildhouses here were the headquarters of powerful local guilds. At 7 Korenlei Het Anker (the Anchor), built in 1739, was the guildhouse of the Tied Boatmen, who had fewer privileges than the occupants of the guildhouse of the Free Boatmen from 1531 at 14 Graslei.

Walk to the Sint-Michielsbrug (St Michael's Bridge) at the end of Korenlei, with its lovely view of the towers of St Nicholas's Church, the Belfry and St Bavo's Cathedral. Cross over to **Sint-Michielskerk** (St Michael's Church). This brings you back to Korenmarkt, for a swift return by tram to the station for the journey back to Bruges.

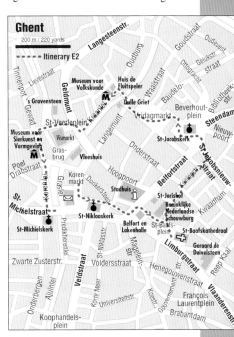

3. OSTEND (OOSTENDE)   *(see maps, p56 & 63)*

You can spend all day doing some or all of this itinerary, which covers the seafront and the old fishermen's quarter behind it. Allow time to sunbathe and swim in warm weather and to dine at one of the many superb seafood restaurants.

To the start: There are direct trains at least hourly between Bruges and Ostend, a 15-minute journey. By road, take the A10 (E40).

From the station, cross the bridge in front of you to the green-hulled **IJslandvaarder** *Amandine* (Iceland Fishing Boat *Amandine*), built in 1961. Her final voyage ended in April 1995 and now this last of Ostend's Iceland-bound trawlers is "moored" permanently in a dry basin in which glass panelling mimics the cold polar sea.

Head north along the waterfront on **Visserskaai** (Fishermen's Wharf), famous for the excellent seafood restaurants on the far side of the street and breezy seafood stalls on the near side that together make this thoroughfare a virtual place of pilgrimage for those who love seafood. If you do nothing else in Ostend, visit one of these and you're sure to bring away good memories.

Sticking to the watery margin, you arrive at the **Noordzeeaquarium** (North Sea Aquarium), to admire its fish, shellfish and sea plants. From here, a few steps bring you to the **Vistrap** (Fish Market), where the day's catch is laid out for popular approval and sale. Cross the street to get a close-up look at two good seafood restaurants, the Old Fisher at No 34 and David Dewaele at No 39,

Above: Albert I Promenade
Right: dish of the day at Fishermen's Wharf

and of the Rubens tavern at No 44, all of which are recommended for your attention, for later if not right away.

Continue into Albert I Promenade and its **Zeeliedengedenkteken** (Seamen's Memorial) across the way, dedicated in 1953 to the naval dead from World War II. Then, turn left into Vlaanderenstraat, to the 19th-century **Ensorhuis** (Ensor House) at No 27, where the Anglo-Belgian painter James Ensor (1860–1949) lived from 1916 until his death. Recently restored, this scarcely distinguished townhouse has a souvenir shop on the ground floor and Ensor's studio on the first.

The Casino and the Beach

Return to the seafront and keep going west. Dull but worthy postwar apartments line this once-fashionable esplanade, replacing the 19th-century mansions that no longer made economic sense – at least, that was the opinion of Ostend at the time. You will quickly appreciate why much of Belgium's coastline is known wryly as the Atlantic Wall, after Hitler's concrete-and-steel coastal defence bunkers.

This brings you to the **Casino-Kursaal**, a 1950s replacement for an 1887 original demolished by the German army to make way for an Atlantic Wall strongpoint. One look at this awesomely ugly Modernist mass will probably be enough to persuade you that Ostend might have done better to have kept the bunker. Work began in 2000 on rebuilding this casino and concert hall in the style that the architect Léon Stijnen had in mind in 1950 – which may or may not constitute an improvement, depending on whom you ask. When the work is completed, some time in 2004, you will be able to visit a brand new panoramic seafront restaurant, a rooftop restaurant, a revamped gaming room and cafes.

You have now arrived at the beach, a long, wide expanse of fine quartz sand. For an idea of what was lost when most 19th-century seafront mansions were demolished, pause for a look at neo-Renaissance Villa Maritza from 1885 at No 76, now an upmarket *belle époque*-style restaurant.

Ostend's Art Galleries

Next along the seafront you come to the 19th-century **Venetiaanse Gaanderijen** (Venetian Galleries). At the entrance to this former royal pavilion stands a sympathetic bronze sculpture, cast in 2000, depicting the late King Baudouin (reigned 1951–93) on foot and wearing a raincoat on a visit to Ostend. Next door to the Galleries, the **Royal Villa** now houses the elegant Oostendse Compagnie Hotel, which includes the equally refined Au Vigneron restaurant. **Koningspark** (King's Park) is at the back.

Albert I Promenade melds into the Zeedijk (Sea Dike) as you come face

Above: windsurfing off Ostend's fine beach

to face with an equestrian statue, created in 1931, of King Leopold II (1865–1909). Here he is depicted gazing out to sea, flanked on either side by Ostend fisherfolk, and being hailed by a Congolese native. For sheer bare-faced effrontery this sculpture takes some beating, when you consider history's recollection of Leopold's notoriously brutish colonial rule over the Congo and his rapacious looting of that country's mineral wealth.

Adjacent to this begin the long, colonnaded **Koninklijke Gaander-ijen** (Royal Galleries), built in 1906 by French architect Charles Girault so that Leopold II and his court could shelter from the wind as they passed along the seafront. The plush Art Deco Thermae Palace Hotel in the centre dates back to 1933. At the far end of the colonnaded gallery, you arrive at the **Wellington Renbaan** (Wellington Racecourse), a horse-racing track for flat, steeplechase and trotting contests built in 1957 to replace a doubtless fancier predecessor that closed during World War II.

Modern Art

Now go east on Koningin Astridlaan and Warschauwstraat to Leopold I Plein and its **equestrian statue** of Leopold I (1831–65), the first King of the Belgians. If you are interested in modern art, you can make a long trek south on Rogierlaan, then sidestep into Romestraat to the **Provinciaal Museum voor Moderne Kunst** (PMMK; Provincial Modern Art Museum; Tues–Sat 10am–6pm). In this converted Modernist department store from

1953 you can see mainly Belgian works by the likes of Panamarenko and Jan Fabre, as well as temporary exhibitions of international art.

Now head for Leopold Park, to stroll among its manicured lawns and flowerbeds, cross the little bridges over its ponds, and check the time on the floral clock at its eastern end. Outside the park, in the middle of Leopold II Laan, you cannot easily miss a renowned Ostend 'personality', officially called *De Zee (The Sea)* but more popularly known as *Dikke Matille (Fat Matilda)*, a sculpture of a reclining, generously endowed woman in all her birthday-suit glory.

Above: outside the Venetian Galleries
Right: Leopold II looks out to sea

Take Witte Nonnenstraat to Wapenplein, a square with a wrought iron band-stand dating back to 1895 situated in its centre. On the square's southern rim you find the redoubtable **Stedelijk Feest-en-Kultuurpaleis** (Municipal Festival and Cultural Palace), which looks something like a design prototype for George Orwell's Ministry of Truth, and which is home to the **Museum voor Schone Kunsten** (Fine Arts Museum; Wed–Mon 10am–noon and 2–5pm), a theatre, a library, and the *diskotheek* – the latter might sound like a 1970s dance venue but in actual fact it's just an audio library. Check out the attached **Beiaardtoren** (Bell Tower), which has a tinkling carillon that's a modern take on an old Flemish tradition.

Art Deco Shopping Gallery

Now is a good time to divert a short way north on Vlaanderenstraat and turn left into the **James Ensorgaanderijen**. This 1930s Art Deco shopping gallery is interesting in itself and has an Ostend pearl at its heart: the Old Flemish **James** tavern at No 34. To sample its homemade shrimp croquettes alone would warrant a considerable detour.

Continue to the end of Kerkstraat and the sanctuary of **Sint-Petrus-en-Pauluskerk** (Church of SS Peter and Paul), a colossal heap of stone and masonry that looks like one of Europe's great centuries-old Gothic master-pieces, but is in fact a century-old neo-Gothic pastiche. However, as pastiches go it's impressive and houses the sumptuous tomb of Belgium's first queen, Marie-Louise of Orléans, who died in Ostend in 1850.

You reach the end of the road by taking Dekenijstraat to Vindictivelaan and the big **Jachthaven** (Yacht Harbour), in which floats the three-masted schooner *Mercator*, a merchant marine training ship that spends most of its time here as a floating museum. Circling the harbour brings you back to Ostend railway station.

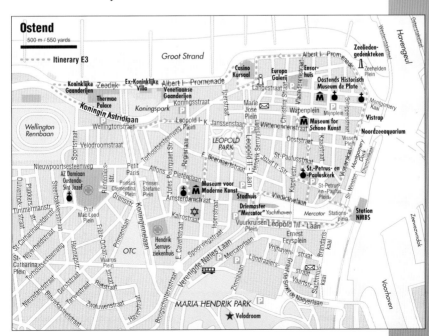

4. YPRES (IEPER) *(see maps, p56, 66 & below)*

A day-long excursion to the town of Ypres. A phoenix risen from the ashes, this historic cloth town was painstakingly rebuilt after being shelled to extinction during World War I. The surrounding Flanders fields, strewn with 185 military cemeteries, have become synonymous with that war's senseless slaughter.

To the start: Ypres is 45km (28 miles) southwest of Bruges. There are trains from Bruges at least hourly; journey time about 1 hour; you usually need to change at Kortrijk. By car, the quickest route is A17 (E403) south to the Kortrijk junction, then A19 west.

From the railway and bus station on René Colaertplein, take Stationsstraat and Tempelstraat, into Boterstraat, and on the right side of the street you will pass the **Oude Vismarkt** (Old Fish Market). You now enter **Grote Markt**, where the giant Gothic extravaganza on the left side of the square is the **Lakenhalle** (Cloth Hall), built 1250–1304, with its east wing added in 1376–8. This is version two though, a pristine replica mostly from the 1920s but finished in 1967; the original was blown apart by German guns in World War I. The Flemish Renaissance building at the east end is the **Stadhuis** (Town Hall).

Above: In Flanders Field Museum

In Flanders Fields

You can get a great view over Ypres and the old theatre of war beyond – providing you're willing to climb 264 steps to the summit of the Cloth Hall's **Belfort** (Belfry) tower, 70m (230ft) high and containing a 49-bell carillon. The **In Flanders Fields Museum** (tel: 057-228584; Apr–Sept: daily 10am–6pm; Oct–Mar: Tues–Sun 10am–5pm) in the Cloth Hall is a superb, interactive insight into the four years of devastation to which the Ypres area was subjected during World War I.

Across the north side of the Grote Markt is **Sint-Martenskathedraal** (St Martin's Cathedral). This rebuilt 13th-century Gothic church, like the Cloth Hall and Belfry, is a testimonial to the wealth and prestige of Ypres during its medieval heyday. Across Vandepeereboomplein, **St George's Memorial Church** in Elverdingsestraat was made into a shrine to the memory of their lost comrades by British and Commonwealth survivors, and it is filled with mementoes of sacrifice. Colourful wall-mounted banners and the pew kneelers are decorated with corps and regimental badges.

Return to the Grote Markt and leave by the eastern end, on Meensestraat, to reach the **Meensepoort** (Menin Gate), also known as the Missing Memorial – inscribed on it are the names of nearly 55,000 British soldiers with no known grave who fell around Ypres between 1914 and 15 August, 1917. Every evening at 8 o'clock, traffic through the gate stops for two minutes while Ypres firefighters play *The Last Post* on silver bugles. Adjacent is a memorial to the more than 43,000 Australians killed in the Ypres salient.

Old Walls and Museums

Turn south along the west bank of the Kasteelgracht, part of the moat around Ypres' 17th-century walls and **Casemates**, now a pleasant park. You can see **Sint-Jacobskerk** (St James's Church) down in Guido Gezelleplein as you pass by, but there's very little good reason for taking a closer look. Right next to the **Rijselsepoort** (Lille Gate), the Ramparts Cemetery is a tranquil British military cemetery with 193 graves. On leaving the ramparts at the city gate, go north for a short distance on Ieperleestraat to the **Stedelijk Museum** (Municipal Museum; Tues–Sat 10am–12.30pm and 2–5pm), which contains paintings and other mementoes from the town's history. Passing through the courtyard of Sint-Jan Godshuis, in which the museum is housed, you emerge into Rijselsestraat once more and turn left.

This takes you past **Sint-Pieterskerk** (St Peter's Church) and leads to the **Merghelynck Museum**, which is just a few steps down a side street at

2A Merghelynckstraat, located in a rebuilt mansion, housing 18th-century furniture and paintings; and the **Belle Godshuis Museum** (Apr–Oct: Tues–Sun 10am–12.30pm and 2–6pm) in a 1276 almshouse (rebuilt), which also has works by local artists. More appealing perhaps, is the **Ter Posterie** cafe/restaurant down a narrow alley at No 57, offering basic Flemish food and 250 Belgian beers, including the local Poperings Hommelbier.

Around the Ypres Salient

If you have your own transport, you can take this short trip out of town to visit World War I sites. Drive to the Menen Gate, go straight on Zonnebeekseweg for a short way, then turn right on Meenseweg (N8). After about 3km (2 miles), just before the **Bellewaerde** theme park, go right on Canadalaan, where you see signs for **Sanctuary Wood** and **Hill 62**. The Sanctuary Wood Museum stands beside one of the few remaining stretches of trenches, shellholes and shattered trees in the Ypres Salient and has photographs and military equipment. Hill 62, the scene of bitter fighting by Canadian troops in 1916, is crowned by the Canadian Memorial.

Return to the N8, go back towards Ypres for about 0.5km (500yds) to the N37 and turn right towards Zonnebeke. A little way beyond Zonnebeke, at Broodseinde, go left on the N303 for about a kilometre (½ mile), then left again to the **Tyne Cot Commonwealth Military Cemetery**. Watched over by a Cross of Remembrance are 12,000 graves of British, Canadian and Anzac soldiers who fell in the Battle of Passchendaele in 1917.

Return to the village crossroads in Zonnebeke, where you go right for 6km (4 miles), including a very brief stretch on the N313, to Langemark. Drive straight through the village and out the other side to the **Deutscher Soldatenfriedhof** (German Soldiers' Cemetery), where 44,000 soldiers are buried in multiple graves, among them members of the Student Regiments killed in the 1914 'Massacre of the Innocents'. From Langemark you return to the N313 for a straight run back to Ypres.

Around Ypres

3 km / 2 miles

---- Itinerary E4

Above: commemorating the fallen
Right: Sanctuary Wood

Leisure Activities

SHOPPING

There are other shops in Bruges than those selling speciality Belgian products such as lace, diamonds, crystal, antiques and handmade pralines, even if it often seems as if there aren't. You find quaintly designed chemists, fashion-conscious boutiques, hardware shops, music shops and video clubs.

Most shops are open Monday to Saturday from 9am to 6pm. Friday evening is *koopavond* (late-shopping evening), when most shops stay open until 8 or 9pm. In summer many shops also open on Sunday for part if not all of the day.

If you are looking for a bargain, the magic words to look for on shop windows are *Solden* (Sales) and *Totale Uitverkoop* (Everything Must Go). Residents of countries outside the European Union may be able to claim back value-added tax (BTW) on purchases in some shops. Those subscribing to the scheme announce this with a sticker on the window or door. It's worth asking, particularly if you buy expensive items.

What to Buy

Lace was once the principal product of Bruges and is certainly the premier souvenir today. In the course of your strolls through Bruges, you are likely to see enough lace shops to satisfy any cravings you have for this ornamental fabric. Most Bruges lace is bobbin lace, made using a 15th-century technique developed in Flanders, where lace was popular as a decorative edging for the clothes of wealthy people. Threads of silk, linen or cotton are crossed and braided around pins. It takes skill to control the hundreds of bobbins – between 300 and 700 – used in the finest *point de fée* (needlepoint) lace. Although most lace on sale in Bruges is machine-made, usually in the Far East, handmade lace in the distinctive *duchesse* (duchess), *bloemenwerk* (flower lace), *rozenkant* (pearled rosary), and *toveresses-*

teek (fairy stitch) styles can still be found. Some shops deal only in the handmade product, which has a Quality Control label and is of course more expensive, while most sell a mix of the two.

Other notable Belgian products to look out for, though most of them are not specific to Bruges, include diamonds, ceramics, crystal (especially the hand-blown products of the Val-St-Lambert workshop in Liège), jewellery from respected modern designers based mostly in Antwerp and Brussels, modern tapestries (like lace, building on the traditions of an art that had almost vanished), and, if you can find them, pewter from Huy, and *Dinanderie*, hand-beaten copper or bronze, from Dinant in the Meuse Valley.

For food and drink products to take home, or just back to your hotel, there is Bruges' own **Oud-Brugge** cheese, as well as others of Belgium's 300 or so different artisanal cheeses; the local beers such as **Straffe Hendrick**, **Brugse Tarwebier**, **Abdij Steenbrugge** and **Brugse Tripel**, and any of the more than 500 Belgian beers; a bottle or two (preferably a stone bottle) of the 270 or so brands of *jenever* (gin) made and sold in Belgium; and handmade chocolate pralines that are positively addictive.

Where to Buy

Expensive upmarket shops, boutiques and department stores mostly occupy the streets lying to the south and west of the Markt, an

Left: lace is the city's leading souvenir
Right: puppets at a weekend market

area that is roughly delimited by **'t Zand**, **Geldmuntstraat-Noordzandstraat** and **Steenstraat-Zuidzandstraat**, and the main streets within it, in particular **Zilverstraat**. **Vlamingstraat**, to the north of the Markt, also has some good shops. You will find no shortage of places selling souvenirs, lace and speciality items all round the city centre. If the weather is inclement you might want to confine yourself to the shopping galleries, such as the **Zilverpand** in Zuidzandstraat, **Ter Steeghere** between Wollestraat and the Burg, **De Gouden Boom** in Wollestraat and the **Simon Stevingalerij** in Simon Stevinplein.

Antiques and Jewellery

Antiek Fimmers-Van der Cruysse
18 Sint-Salvatorskerkhof
Tel: 050-342025
Antiques and domestic silverware.

Brugs Diamanthuis
5 Cordoeaniersstraat
Tel: 050-344160
A beautiful building dating from 1518, which sells a sparkling array of fine diamonds. Tax-free purchases are available for non-European Union residents.

Books

Brugse Boekhandel
2 Dijver
Tel: 050-332952
A centrally located bookshop that stocks a reasonable range of English-language books, including travel guides, as well as newspapers, magazines and maps.

De Reyghere Boekhandel
12 Markt
Tel: 050-334308
Bookshop that sells international newspapers and magazines.

Crafts and Gifts

Argus Keramiek
18 Walplein
Tel: 050-344432
Decorative ceramic wall tiles, many with images of Bruges, and other pottery items.

Callebert
25 Wollestraat
Tel: 050-335061
Setting its face determinedly against the traditional, this shops sells stylish modern gifts – at a stylish modern price.

Kantuweeltje
11 Philipstockstraat
Tel: 050-334225
A lace and tapestry specialist since 1895. Here you can see fine lace pieces being made by hand.

Mozaïek
4 Stoofstraat
Tel: 050-349036
An upmarket gift shop, with a wide range of household and personal items.

Selection
10–12 Breidelstraat
Tel: 050-331186
There are so many lace shops in Bruges that it is difficult to judge them all on quality and price. Selection sells a good range of handmade lace and is centrally located.

Food and Drink

Malesherbes
3–5 Stoofstraat
Tel: 050336924
This is a French delicatessen, with all that implies in terms of taste and range of artisanal products.

Pralinette
31B Wollestraat
Tel: 050-348383
This is the place to find some of the great-

Above: handmade chocolates, a Belgian speciality
Right: the fish market, where raw herring is a popular delicacy

est varieties of chocolates, made with syrup, roasted nuts and fruit fillings.

Van Tilborgh
1B Noordzandstraat
Tel: 050-335904
The owner makes lip-smacking pralines according to her own recipes.

Verheecke
30 Steenstraat
Tel: 050-332286
Some of the finest homemade pralines.

Woolstreet Company
31A Wollestraat
Tel: 050-348383
A wide range of Belgian beers, including the main locally produced brews.

Miscellaneous
Artlux
1 Simon Stevinplein
Tel: 050-336095
Fine leather goods such as handbags and gloves.

De Witte Pelikaan
23 Vlamingstraat
Tel: 050-348284
It's Santa Claus (or Sinterklaas) time all year round in this specialist Christmas shop.

Dille & Kamille
17–18 Simon Stevinplein
Tel: 050-341180
Stocks a wide and interesting range of house-hold products, toys and gifts, including old-fashioned kitchen utensils, soaps, teas, dried flowers and fruits, herbs, spices and plants.

Inno
11–13 Steenstraat
Tel: 050-330603
The city's premier department store.

The Tintin Shop
3 Steenstraat
Tel: 050-334292
Everything you ever wanted to own – including a red-and-white-chequered Moon rocket – from Belgium's most famous comic strip.

Markets
Antiques and Flea Market Dijver (with an extension at the Vismarkt). Mid-March to mid-November, Saturday and Sunday, noon–5pm. In addition to being a source of bargains and fine antiques, the market's scenic setting beside the tree-shaded canal makes this a treat for the eyes.
Markt Wednesday 8am–1pm. General street market in the place that in former times was the city's main market square.
't Zand Saturday 8am–1pm. One side of 't Zand square is called Vrijdagmarkt (Friday Market) because of the big street market that used to take place here on Friday– it is now held on Saturday.
Fish Market Vismarkt, Tuesday–Saturday 8am–1pm. Even if you do not want to buy fish, it is still interesting to see this market, in the purpose-built colonnaded market dating from 1820–21. Raw herring is a popular delicacy here.

EATING OUT

Belgium has more Michelin Star restaurants per capita than France, and Belgian cuisine, firmly based on the country's regional traditions, is a delight to the tastebuds. There is no shortage of eateries in busy, cosmopolitan Bruges and you find restaurants in all price categories all over town. About the only generalisation you can make is that the further you get from the centre and the less dependent on tourists an establishment is, the more likely it is that you'll find genuine Flemish taste and style. But this is far from a hard-and-fast rule, and it's just about impossible to eat a bad meal anywhere here. Restaurants range from the usual fast-food outlets to seriously epicurean establishments, with a vast mid-range of tasteful, moderately priced places.

Firmly Flemish, Bruges restaurants are treasuries of the full range of Belgian cuisine, from traditional Flemish dishes such as *waterzooï op Gentse wijze* (a traditional fish-stew from Ghent – though chicken is more often used nowadays than fish) and *paling in 't groen* (eel in a green herb sauce), to Walloon specialities such as *jambon d'Ardennes* (smoked Ardennes ham) and game.

Belgians love mussels (*mosselen* in Flemish, *moules* in French), and a big steaming pot served with a side dish of *frieten* (french

fries) with mayonnaise is a real treat. The nearby Belgian coast delivers other seafood, such as herring – lightly salted on the boat, and eaten raw as *maatjes* – sole and North Sea shrimps; at Oostduinkerke fishermen still ride into the water on sturdy 'sea-going' horses to harvest them. And don't forget asparagus, chicory (Belgian endive), even the humble Brussels sprout.

The following is a rough price guide for a three-course dinner for one, excluding wine and tip. Lunch menus are generally cheaper, and many restaurants have a good-value *dagschotel* (dish of the day) or a *dagmenu* (menu of the day).

€€€ = over €60
€€ = €30–60
€ = under €30

Bhavani
5 Simon Stevinplein
Tel: 050-339025
Quality authentic Indian cuisine is served here, making this a good place if you want a change from Belgian food. €€

Bistro De Stove
4 Kleine Sint-Amandsstraat
Tel: 050-337835
Less formal than many of the city's better

Above: Bhavani in Simon Stevinplein serves quality Indian meals

restaurants but still quietly elegant, and right up there in the taste stakes, with seafood and Flemish dishes strong on the menu. €€

't Bourgoensche Cruyce
41–3 Wollestraat
Tel: 050-337926
One of the best and most atmospheric dining experiences in Bruges, in a beautiful old restaurant overlooking the canal. French and Belgian regional specialities feature on the fixed-price menu. €€

Brasserie Erasmus
35 Wollestraat
Tel: 050-335781
A great place for informal budget dining. All the speciality dishes are prepared with Belgian beer, of which this cafe/restaurant stocks more than 100 different kinds. €

Breidel-De Coninck
24 Breidelstraat
Tel: 050-339746
A generations-old standard bearer of the fine Belgian art of eating mussels, prepared in numerous ways. Other seafood dishes also find a place on the menu. €€

't Dreveken
10–11 Huidenvettersplein
Tel: 050-339506
It would be hard not to be charmed by the view of the canal at Rozenhoedkaai from this comfortable and welcoming restaurant serving Flemish and seafood dishes. €

Duc de Bourgogne
12 Huidenvettersplein
Tel: 050-332038
A classic Bruges dining experience, albeit a little too tourist-orientated. French dishes are served in baronial surroundings, with a much-photographed canal view. €€€

De Gouden Meermin
31 Markt
Tel: 050-333776
You trade a little in terms of distinguished service and authentic food here in return for a great position on the Markt. Nevertheless, the straightforward menu is well worth sampling. €

Right: fattening but fabulous

De Karmeliet
19 Langestraat
Tel: 050-338259
One of three Belgian restaurants that sport a coveted three Michelin stars (the other two are in Brussels), this smallish place in a patrician house is a temple of fine food and excellent service. Thanks to owner/chef Geert Van Haecke having his feet firmly on the ground, it's not nearly as stuffy as it might be. €€€

Kasteel Minnewater
4 Minnewater
Tel: 050-334254
A real neo-Gothic château with a waterside terrace beside the effortlessly romantic Minnewater (Lake of Love), and if the prices are less than might be expected in such surroundings, the quality is not. €€

Koto
In the Hotel De Medici, 15 Potterierei
Tel: 050-443131
A Japanese restaurant that in typically stylish surroundings serves top-flight *teppan yaki* and classic cuisine such as *sushi, sashimi* and *tempura.* €€€

Lotus
5 Wapenmakersstraat
Tel: 050-331078
The hallowed atmosphere at this vegetarian restaurant just north of the Burg may be somewhat at odds with the diners' evident need to grab a quick bite at lunchtime, but this a haven of fine food and a good choice for lunch. €€

Maximilian van Oostenrijk
17 Wijngaardplein
Tel: 050-334723
In about as touristy a location as you can get in Bruges, in the square beside the Begijnhof, Maximilian's serves tasty Flemish specialities like *waterzooï* (fish or chicken stew) and *paling* (eel), as well as good mussels. €–€€

Pietje Pek
13 Sint-Jacobstraat
Tel: 050-347874
Behind its Art Nouveau facade, this traditional restaurant offers satisfying portions of its speciality cheese and meat fondues, plus an eat-all-you-want menu. €–€€

De Snippe
53 Nieuwe Gentweg
Tel: 050-337070
Flemish and French dishes, from a menu that's strong on seafood and game in season, are served here in the dining room of an 18th-century mansion converted into a hotel. €€€

De Visscherie
8 Vismarkt
Tel: 050-330212
Its name and location in the Fish Market are more than a hint that the speciality is seafood, and no one does it better. Nouvelle and classic cuisine in elegant surroundings. €€€

Damme
De Lieve
10 Jacob van Maerlantstraat
Tel: 050-356630
This fine restaurant remains a stalwart performer amid Damme's fading claim to be a culinary stronghold. Specialises in seasonal Belgian and French cuisine. €€–€€€

Pallieter
12 Kerkstraat
Tel 050-354675
An atmospheric place with a half-timbered ceiling; its speciality is saddle of lamb Dijonnaise. €–€€

Ghent
't Buikske Vol
17 Kraanlei
Tel: 09-225 1880
One of Ghent's favourite chefs, Peter Vyncke, puts his highly individual stamp on seafood and adventurous Flemish and French dishes. Cosy and intimate, it delivers excellent value for money. €€

Vier Tafels
6 Plotersgracht
Tel: 09-225 0525
In the heart of the medieval Patershol district, this restaurant serves up not only Flemish delicacies, but also an intriguing range of world cuisine, with such ingredients as reindeer, ostrich, kangaroo and crocodile. €€

Brasserie Pakhuis
4 Schuurkenstraat
Tel: 09-223 5555
Perhaps a little too conscious of its own modish good looks, this Franco-Italian brasserie is in a restored warehouse, with cast iron pillars and wrought-iron balustrades. When it comes to taste, it delivers, and the oyster and seafood platters are noteworthy. €€

Ostend
Old Fisher
34 Visserskaai
Tel: 059-501768
Standards and quality come and go on this street beside the fishing harbour that's lined with seafood restaurants. This one has maintained a steady presence and might well be the best moderately priced seafood restaurant in town. €€

Villa Maritza
76 Albert I Promenade
Tel: 059-508808
Housed in an opulently furnished and decorated *belle époque* villa with sea view. Serves Belgian cuisine to a high standard. Seafood features strongly on the menu. €€€

Ypres
De Waterpoort
43 Brugseweg
Tel: 057-205452
This stylish restaurant, furnished in a spare modern fashion and with a garden terrace, is several blocks north of the Grote Markt, beyond the moat. It serves updated versions of Flemish dishes and seafood. €–€€

NIGHTLIFE

Bruges is far from being a hot nightspot. Visitors have already walked their socks off during the day touring its many sights, so when it comes to stepping out after dark most can only hobble as far as the nearest restaurant. The city is not one of Belgium's cultural citadels, but a small provincial town that struck tourist gold thanks to its history and beauty. The big-name orchestras, opera and ballet companies are based in Brussels, Antwerp, Ghent and Liège and though they occasionally visit, that's not quite the same thing. In addition, there is no university and few institutes of higher education to create the kind of happy-hour animation that students excel at generating. There are some fairly discreet sex clubs, though not a well-defined red-light district.

All is not dark, though, when the sun goes down and if you want to experience the city as more than just one big museum, one of the best ways is to get active. For comprehensive information on what's going on in the city, pick up the free, multilingual monthly brochure *Events@Brugge* and the free monthly newspaper *Exit* (in Dutch, but venue details and dates are easy to follow), from the tourist office, hotels and venues.

To sit on a canalside cafe terrace drinking a Belgian beer is to touch the heart of the Bruges experience. If you want to drink a local beer, look out for those from De Halve Maan and De Gouden Boom breweries. The former produces the strong and popular Straffe Hendrik beer; the latter the equally popular 'white' Brugse Tarwebier, strong Brugse Tripel and Abdij Steenbrugge.

If you make the excursion suggested in this book to Ghent, just 20 minutes away by train, you may have time to take in some of that city's more lively nightlife scene.

Classical Music and Theatre

Concertgebouw
't Zand
Tel: 050-476999
The ultra-modern Concertgebouw was unveiled in 2002 to give Bruges a concert and opera hall worthy of the city's international stature.

Koninklijke Stadsschouwburg (Royal Municipal Theatre)
29 Vlamingstraat
Tel: 050-443060
This theatre is still a venue for opera, classical music, drama and dance, but has been eclipsed by the Concertgebouw.

Theater De Biekorf
3 Kuipersstraat
Tel: 050-443060
Performances at this modern theatre are almost always in Dutch.

Above: Duke's Jazz Bar, Hotel Navarra

Carillon Concerts
Belfry, Markt
Tel: 050-334073

The city *carilloneur* or a guest player climbs up the inside of the Belfry to the carillon keyboard and starts to play. From the cafe terraces of the square below – indeed from all over the city – you can hear the 47-bell carillon in concert from mid-June to October on Monday, Wednesday and Saturday 9–10pm, Sunday 2.15–3pm; September to mid-June on Wednesday, Saturday and Sunday 2.15–3pm.

Festival of Flanders

Bruges always hosts a number of events from the festival, which is a season of cultural events that take place in cities throughout the Flanders region. Recitals are often held at Holy Saviour Cathedral, and St James's, Our Lady of the Blind, Our Lady of the Pottery, St Walburga's, and other churches, and at the Stedelijk Muziekconservatorium, 23–25 Sint-Jakobsstraat.

Medieval Banquet

Brugge Anno 1468
86 Vlamingstraat (the former Sacred Heart church)
Tel: 050-347572

Dip into the spirit of the Middle Ages, courtesy of Celebrations Entertainment, while ploughing your way through trencherman quantities of meat, cheese and bread, washed down by traditional ales. Thrill to actors playing the parts of aristocrats, knights, falconers, jesters, minstrels, dancers and witches to 'recreate' the wedding of Duke Charles the Bold of Burgundy to Margaret of York in 1468. Performances are staged April to October, Thursday to Saturday 7.30 to 10pm; November to March, Saturday 7.30 to 10pm.

Bars and Cafes

't Brugs Beertje
5 Kemelstraat
Tel: 050-339616

The city's most popular beer cafe, offering a range of 300 brews, most of them Belgian. The owner gives pre-booked group seminars on Belgian beer and beer culture in English, French, German and Dutch.

De Craenenburg
16 Markt
Tel: 050-333402

You may want to spend some time after dark in one of the cafes around the Markt, drinking in the romantic scenery as well as the Belgian beer. This cafe/restaurant in a former residence of the knights of the counts of Flanders is a good choice.

't Dreupelhuisje
9 Kemelstraat
Tel: 050-342421

Belgium's 70 distilleries produce 270 brands of *jenever*, a stiff grain-spirit served in small, brimful glasses. This cramped *jenever* and liqueur specialist stocks a hundred (fierce) examples of the art. Look out for such popular Flemish brands as Filliers Oude Graanjenever, De Poldenaar Oude Antwerpsche, Van Damme and Sint-Pol.

Music Cafés & Clubs

Charlie Rockets
19 Hoogstraat
Tel: 050-330660

This is a bright and breezy American bar that appeals particularly to a young crowd. There are American and Belgian beers as well as bourbon and cocktails, music – swing, soul, jazz, rhythm and blues – and pool tables, amid a decor of traffic lights, petrol pumps and street signs. Serves Tex-Mex food and American breakfast. Open from 8am to 4am.

Ma Ricca Rokk
7–8 't Zand
Tel: 050-338358

This music cafe is noisy enough to appeal to youthful spirits, especially those who can handle techno while they are drinking.

L'Obcédé
11 't Zand
Tel: 050-347171

Pop music from the 1970s to the present.

Du Phare
2 Sasplein
Tel: 050-343590

Occasional live jazz and blues bands play here; popular with locals.

De Versteende Nacht
11 Langestraat
Tel: 050-343293
You can have a meal here, read strip cartoon books (in Dutch), have a drink, and listen to jazz – from bebop to modern.

Vino Vino
15 Grauwwerkersstraat
Tel: 050-345115
If you like Spanish tapas and are a fan of the Blues, this unlikely mixture is Vino Vino's stock-in-trade.

Ghent
Opera
De Vlaamse Opera
3 Schouwburgstraat
Tel: 09-225 2425
Superb 19th-century hall features both Belgian and international opera companies.

Classical Music
Stedelijke Concertzaal De Bijloke
2 Jozef Kluyskensstraat
Tel: 09-233 6878
The city's premier venue for classical music.

Theatre
Koninklijke Nederlandse Schouwburg
17 Sint-Baafsplein
Tel: 09-225 0101
Most performances are in Dutch, of course, but there is simultaneous translation in English and French, via cordless headphones.

Bars and Cafes
Bier Academie
50 Vrijdagmarkt
Tel: 09-233 4251
The city's oldest cafe (also known as Dulle Griet) is popular with students who have a tradition of downing potent Kwak beer, from a round-bottomed glass held up by a wooden frame – it's easy to find yourself with a similar requirement after drinking a few.

't Dreupelkot
12 Groentenmarkt
Tel: 09-224 2120
Specialises in *jenever*, and occupies a cosy old cafe beside the River Leie.

Het Galgenhuisje
5 Groentemarkt
Tel: 09-233 4251
Tiny cafe where it is easy to meet local people. There's a traditional Flemish restaurant downstairs in the cellar.

Het Waterhuis aan de Bierkant
9 Groentenmarkt
Tel: 09-225-0680
A very popular bar with a pleasant waterside location, with more than 100 different Belgian beers. Try a glass of Ghent's own Stopken beer.

Ostend
Casino-Kursaal
Oosthelling
Tel: 059-705111
Come here to play roulette and blackjack, to dine out in the fine restaurant, or to take in a concert.

Ypres
Ter Posterie
57 Rijsselsestraat
Tel: 057-200580
Some 200 beers, among them rarely spotted brands from the small breweries of West Flanders, are on the drinks list in this farmhouse-style tavern.

Right: try a glass of Straffe Hendrik

CALENDAR OF EVENTS

January

Snow and Ice Sculpture Festival (December and first week January): *See details under December, opposite.*

Polar Bears in the North Sea, Ostend (first Sunday after New Year): Try it if you dare. The first dip of the year in the North Sea. Free soup and *jenever* (gin) for participants (tel: 059-701199).

March

Dead Rat Ball, Ostend (first Saturday): An outrageous fancy-dress ball, held at the Casino-Kursaal, that takes its name from a Montmartre cabaret. The proceeds go to charity (tel: 059-701199).

April

Floraliën Flower Show, Ghent (every five years, next in 2005): Belgium's premier flower show (tel: 09-267 7114).

Flower Fair, Ypres (Easter Monday): Flowers galore in the Grote Markt (tel: 057-207683).

May

Procession of the Holy Blood (Ascension Day, Thursday 40 days after Easter; variable): This colourful ceremony dates back to 1291 and celebrates the raising up of Jesus into heaven 40 days after the Resurrection. The Relic of the Holy Blood is led through the streets by the Bishop of Bruges, and residents in Burgundian and biblical costumes follow in procession, acting out historical and biblical events along the way. These recall the story (or legend) of Count Thierry of Alsace bringing the precious relic from the Holy Land to Bruges in 1149 after the Second Crusade, as well as incidents from both the Old and New Testaments and the Passion of Christ. Finally, two prelates carry the golden shrine containing the relic, preceded by the members of the Noble Confraternity of the Holy Blood and other religious associations. The procession begins and ends at the Chapel of the Holy Blood (tel: 050-448686).

Kattestoet (Festival of the Cats), Ypres (every three years, second Sunday in May; next in 2006): This colourful pageant witnesses hundreds of cats being thrown from the Belfry by the town jester. The custom dates back centuries to when cats who kept the Cloth Hall free of mice eventually outlived their usefulness. Unwanted, the felines were disposed of by throwing them off the Belfry. Animal lovers can relax – in these enlightened times the cats are made of velvet. The pageant includes a procession through the town of 'giants' that resemble Muppets on steroids (tel: 057-228584).

Above: a Wijngaardplein watering hole, but not for humans

July

Festival of Flanders – Bruges Early Music Festival (late July to early August): Three weeks of themed early classical music, in concert halls and historic churches (tel: 050-332283).

Cactus Festival (three days, first or second week): World music festival in Minnewater Park features both both big and not-so-big international names (tel: 050-332014).

Axion Beach Rock Festival, Zeebrugge (mid-month): Non-stop music from 10am to 3am the next morning on the beach (tel: 050-545042).

Gentse Feesten (Ghent Festivities; last week): A time of music, dancing, and fun and games throughout the city (tel: 09-239 4260).

August

Festival of Flanders – Bruges Early Music Festival (first week): See details under entry in July.

Canal Festival (this lasts for six non-consecutive days from mid-month, every three years: next one scheduled for 2004). This triennial celebration of the city's *reien* (canals) and history began in 1959. The festivities take place in the evening and offer a combination of historical tableaux, dancing, open-air concerts, as well as plenty of opportunities for eating and drinking (tel: 050-448686).

Sand Sculpture Festival, Zeebrugge (mid-month to mid-September): International sculptors work in sand on the beach (tel: 050-545042).

Book Fair, Damme (1 week, mid-month): The main open presentation in Bruges' neighbouring community, which is known as the Village of Books (tel: 050-353319).

Lacemaker Days (mid-month): Demonstrations of lace-making (and lace sales) in Walplein (tel: 050-330072).

Procession of Our Lady of Blindekens (15th, Feast of the Assumption): A costumed procession from this church, carrying its 14th-century gilded silver statue of the Madonna and Child, goes from here to Our Lady of the Pottery Church (tel: 050-310545).

Praalstoet van de Gouden Boom (Golden Tree Pageant; every five years; the next is in 2007): Although it only dates back to 1958, the quinquennial pageant recalls the sumptuous marriage of Duke of Burgundy Charles the Bold to Margaret of York in 1468, when a great procession and tournament was held in the Markt (tel: 050-448686).

September

Sand Sculptures Festival, Zeebrugge Description under August, above.

Festival of Flanders – Ghent Classical and World Music Festival (early September to late October): Ghent's share of the regional arts festival unfolds in concert halls, churches and other venues (tel: 09-243 9494).

Heritage Weekend (first or second week): Bruges adopts a different national heritage theme each year (tel: 050 448686).

October

Festival of Flanders – Ghent Classical and World Music Festival (first three weeks): See details under entry in September.

Flanders International Film Festival, Ghent (10 days, mid-month): An event that has grown in stature over the past three decades to become one of Europe's premier movie showcases (tel: 09-221 8946).

International Art & Antiques Fair (one week, end of month): Features a wealth of paintings, from the late Middle Ages to the 19th century, along with European period furniture, Asian art, and *objets d'art*, sculpture and other items from around the world. Markt (tel: 050-354007).

November

Armistice Day Commemoration, Ypres (11th): Various events at military cemeteries and other monuments recall the 11th hour of the 11th day of the 11th month in 1918, when the guns fell silent on the Western Front (tel: 057-228584).

December

Snow and Ice Sculpture Festival (entire month, and first week January): During December, the big square in front of Bruges railway station becomes the setting for an open-air gallery for really 'cool' artists (tel: 050-550905).

Practical
Information

GETTING THERE

By Air

Brussels National Airport, 14km (8 miles) from Brussels, is the closest international airport to Bruges. The airport is served by direct flights by the Belgian airline SN Brussels Airlines (www.brussels-airlines.com) and international airlines from cities in the UK, North America, most European capitals and other important cities around the world.

Three trains an hour depart from the airport station to Brussels' Gare du Nord, Gare Centrale and Gare du Midi stations; journey time to Gare Centrale is 20 minutes. Trains for Bruges depart from all three stations. A taxi from the airport to Gare Centrale costs about €35.

By Sea

Dunkerque and Calais in France, and Zeebrugge on Belgium's coast are the nearest passenger ferry ports. Calais is served from Dover by Hoverspeed (UK, tel: 0870 2408070; Belgium, tel: 02-710 6444; www.hoverspeed.com) on car-carrying jet catamarans. Zeebrugge is served from Hull by P&O Ferries (UK, tel: 08705 202020; Belgium, tel: 050-543411; www.poferries.com) on overnight car ferry; every two days from Rosyth near Edinburgh by Superfast Ferries (UK, tel: 0870 234 0870; Belgium, tel: 050-252292; www.superfast.com).

By Rail

Bruges railway station (tel: 050-382382, 6.30am–10.30pm) is at Stationsplein, 1.6km (1 mile) south of the city centre. Look for 'Brugge' on the station destination boards. There are frequent services from Brussels (1 hour), Ghent and Antwerp (both 15 minutes), and from Zeebrugge. There is also a service to and from Lille in northern France, connecting with the Eurostar (UK, tel: 08705 186186; www. eurostar.com) from London and the TGV from Paris. From Paris you can also take the Thalys (www. thalys.com) high-speed train via Brussels direct to Bruges, and slower, cheaper Euro-City (EC) trains, changing in Brussels. The international (INT) train from Cologne to London, via Ostend, stops in Bruges. From Amsterdam, you travel via Antwerp and Brussels on either the Thalys or on regular international and inter-city trains.

By Bus

Eurolines (UK, tel: 0990 808080; Belgium, tel: 02-203 0707; www.eurolines.com) operate services from London's Victoria Coach Station, via Eurotunnel, to Bruges bus station, next to the railway station.

By Car

You can reach Bruges from Brussels and Ostend on the E40 (A10), Zeebrugge on the N17, or via the French ferry ports and the Channel Tunnel (UK, tel: 08705 353535; www.eurotunnel.com) on the E40 (A1 in France, then A18 and A10 in Belgium).

TRAVEL ESSENTIALS

When to Visit

Between April and October the weather is generally fine and museums and other

Left: a great way to get around
Right: the town's railway station

attractions are open longer than during the rest of the year, but Bruges can get extremely crowded during this period, particularly during July and August and at weekends, and hotel rooms and restaurant reservations are hard to come by. Spring and autumn are good times to visit. The city is far less busy in winter, and the wet, grey days somehow suit its mouldering medieval character; and if you are very lucky, you might be able to skate on the canals. Be aware that most of the town's museums close on Mondays.

Visas & Passports

EU citizens do not need a passport or visa but must have an ID card (as the UK has no ID card, a passport is still necessary for its citizens). No visa is required for citizens of most European countries, the US, Canada, Australia, New Zealand, Japan and some other countries. If in doubt, check with the Belgian embassy or consulate in your country of departure, or with your travel agent.

Customs

There are no currency limitations, incoming or outgoing. For travellers arriving from another EU country there are no duty-free allowances. Import of items for personal use are essentially unlimited, but you may be asked to account for having more than 3,200 cigarettes, 400 cigars, or 400g tobacco; 90 litres of wine; 10 litres of spirits; and unusually large amounts of other goods. Travellers from a non-EU country can import duty-free 200 cigarettes, or 50 cigars, or 50g tobacco; 2 litres of wine, or 1 litre of spirits.

Weather

Generally, the climate is temperate. In July and August it can be hot and humid, but as Bruges is fairly close to the North Sea, rain is never rare. Winters are usually mild, with periods of snow. Average summer temperature is 16°C (60°F), though it can soar to 30°C (86°F); the winter average is 3°C (37°F), but sometimes goes below freezing.

Clothing

You would be well advised to pack a sweater or cardigan, even in summer, because evenings may be cool. An umbrella is vital almost any time. Warm clothes are needed in winter. In most situations, including the opera and dining out, casual clothes are perfectly acceptable.

Electricity

The unit of electricity is 220 volts AC. Hotels may have a 110-volt outlet for shavers.

Time Differences

Belgium is on Central European Standard Time, with Daylight Saving Time from late March to late October. This is GMT plus one hour in winter and plus two hours in summer. Belgium is one hour ahead of the UK and six hours ahead of US Eastern Standard Time (though the dates when daylight saving time begins and ends may vary by a week or so between Europe and North America).

GETTING ACQUAINTED

Geography

Bruges lies on the edge of the Flemish polderland 88km (55 miles) northwest of Brussels, 92km (57 miles) west of Antwerp, 46km (28 miles) northwest of Ghent, and 24km (15 miles) south of the Channel ferry port of Ostend, which is located roughly at the midpoint of Belgium's 64-km (40-mile) North Sea coast.

Economy

Tourism, transport and distribution, and light manufacturing are the main sources of income. Zeebrugge's port is expanding rapidly and winning an increasing share of western Europe's maritime trade, and Bruges benefits as an important trans-shipment centre for canal and rail traffic.

Religion

Belgium is a Catholic country. If attendance at Sunday Mass is anything to go by, nowadays Catholicism seems to be honoured more in the breach than the observance.

Etiquette

Don't reply in French if a local speaks to you in English. Tip the canal-boat pilot and the horse-and-carriage driver (they won't be seriously offended if you don't, but they will be slightly miffed).

practical information

Whom Do You Trust?

Not someone who tries to sell you the Belfry carillon bells, of course. On a very minor level, the potted histories you hear on canal-boat and horse-and-carriage tours don't always pass the test of historical exactitude. But if you can't trust someone from squeaky clean Bruges, who can you trust? There is anecdotal evidence that some hotel and restaurant staff take tourists for granted and provide less-than-trustworthy (and less-than-friendly) service, but this can be a risk in any popular tourist area.

Population

The total population of the metropolitan area, including neighbouring *gemeenten* (districts), is 120,000. Compared with Brussels and other Flemish cities such as Ghent and Antwerp, the population of Bruges is more homogeneous; there are noticeably fewer ethnic minority residents.

MONEY MATTERS

Currency

Belgium's currency is the euro (€), comprised of 100 cents. There are six euro bank notes: 5, 10, 20, 50, 100 and 500 euros; and eight euro coins: 1 cent, 2 cents, 5 cents, 10 cents, 20 cents and 50 cents, and 1 and 2 euros.

Bruges has no American Express or Thomas Cook office. Banks give the best exchange rates for foreign currency, while the exchange desk at Toerisme Brugge also gives fair deals.

Credit Cards

The main international credit and charge cards are accepted by many businesses. Travellers' cheques can be exchanged for euros at banks and foreign exchange offices or, as a last resort, at hotels.

Cash Machines

There are cash machines called 'Bancontact' and 'Mister Cash' at many points in the city centre. These can be accessed by foreign bank cards and credit cards linked to the international Cirrus and Plus networks; some also serve major charge-card holders. BBL Bank, 18 Markt, has a single ATM that is convenient but often busy.

Tipping

Bills for taxis, restaurants, hotels and hairdressers include a 16 percent service charge. Staff still appreciate a tip of 5–10 percent for good service, though you won't be publicly humiliated for not leaving one. Toilet attendants will make your visit a misery if you fail to leave about €0.25.

Taxes

Value-added tax (BTW) on most goods and services is a hefty 21.5 percent, and 6 percent on hotel bills. Residents of non-EU countries can recover most of the higher rate from shops that subscribe to a Tax-Free Shopping programme – look for a sticker on the window and ask for details.

GETTING AROUND

Bruges is small enough and rewarding enough to see entirely on foot, but wear comfortable shoes because those picturesque cobblestones can be heavy going. Watch out for bicycles, which you may not hear coming up behind you, or from blind corners, until they are almost upon you.

Bicycle

Traffic control measures have made cyclists privileged road users, and in more than 50 of the narrow, one-way streets in the centre they can travel in both directions. Many hotels offer bikes for hire. So also does the railway station (cheapest if you have a valid

Left: best foot forward

railway ticket to Bruges) from the station's Baggage Depot, tel: 050-302329. Other places to hire bikes are 't Koffieboontje, 4 Hallestraat; Eric Popelier, 14 Hallestraat; De Ketting, 23 Gentpoortstraat; and Bauhaus Bike Rental, 135 Langestraat. Cycle carefully, because the streets are crowded with pedestrians, many of whom have little experience of dealing with bikes and are liable to step out in front of you.

Bus

The main city bus stations are at Stationsplein outside the railway station, and at the big square called 't Zand southwest of the centre. In the centre many buses stop at or near the Markt. Schedules are prominently displayed. A one-day pass for unlimited travel on all city buses can be bought at the kiosks outside Bruges Station and at 't Zand, or on the bus. For city and regional bus information, tel: 0800 13663.

Car

Bruges has taken steps to block the flow of private cars through the city centre. Cars are funnelled onto one of five one-way roads leading to and from the ring road. Illegally parked cars, or cars that have outstayed their welcome at a meter, stand a good chance of being clamped or towed away. Preferably leave your car in your hotel car park or at one of the four free car parks near the railway station. There are six paid underground car parks (NAPARC, tel: 050-339030) dotted around the centre and clearly signposted, though these get expensive for long stays, and free street-parking outside the centre.

Only hire a car for excursions out of Bruges. Hertz is at 6 Baron Ruzettelaan, tel: 050-377234; Avis is at 97/7 Koningin Astridlaan, tel: 050-394451.

Sightseeing Tours

The best way to see Bruges is from the open-topped tour-boats that ply the waterways daily from 10am to 6pm between March and mid-November, and on weekends and public holidays, also in holiday periods in winter (ice permitting). They give an unforgettable view of the old city and trips last about half an hour.

Another good way to see the sights is by horse-drawn carriage, leaving from the Markt (from the Burg on Wednesday morning). Horse-drawn trams also do the rounds. Den Oekden Peerdentram (tel: 050-344182) leaves from 't Zand starting at 9am; tours last 30 minutes. Firmin's Paardentram (tel: 050-336136) leaves from the Markt starting at 9am; tours last 45 minutes.

A 50-minute minibus tour of the city departs every hour daily between 10am and 4–7pm, depending on the month. Contact Sightseeing Line, 5 Paul Gilsonstraat, tel: 050-355024. The same company runs excursions to Damme, going there by bus and returning on the paddle steamer *Lamme Goedzaak*.

If you'd rather walk, the tourist office can arrange a guide. In July and August you can join a daily guided tour at 3pm from the tourist office. 'Walkman' guides with taped details in English are available from Toerisme Brugge. They also produce *5 Times Bruges by Bike*, giving details of routes in the city. For mountain-bike tours in the countryside around Bruges, contact Back Road Bikes, tel: 050-330775.

Taxi

The main taxi stands are at the Markt, tel: 050-334444, and at Stationsplein outside the railway station, tel: 050-384660.

HOURS & HOLIDAYS

Business Hours

The main museums are open every day except Monday 9.30am–5pm. Churches and smaller museums generally have more restricted opening times, including a lunch break and closing days, usually Saturday and/or Sunday, and Tuesday or Wednesday in winter.

Left: a City Tour bus flies the flags

Regular banking hours are Monday to Friday from 9am–5pm (some banks remain open until 7pm on Thursday evening). Shops are generally open from Monday to Saturday 9am–6pm, with opening until 9pm on Friday. Many shops, particularly those in the tourist trade – which means almost all of them – are also open on Sunday.

Public Holidays
New Year 1 January
Easter Monday variable date
Labour Day 1 May
Ascension Day 6th Thursday after Easter
Pentecost Monday 7th Monday after Easter
National Day 21 July
Assumption 15 August
All Saints 1 November
Armistice 11 November
Christmas 25 December

ACCOMMODATION

Hotels
Unlike in modern cities with hotels that are by and large more concerned with their own sense of style, or lack of it, in Bruges your hotel will almost certainly be a genuine complement to the city's sense of its history and worth. There are few de luxe but soulless, business-only establishments and equally few sleazy joints at the bottom end. Whatever their star-rating, all the lodgings recommended here have something that sets them apart from even the generally excellent run of their peers.

There is no shortage of hotels, but because the town also has no shortage of visitors, it may seem as if there is. You find a good choice in all categories, from luxury to budget, and so long as you book well in advance and it's not one of the peak periods, you'll probably get what you want.

If you trust to serendipity and arrive with no place to stay, go straight to the tourist office *(see page 90),* which can almost guarantee to find you something. At all periods you have a better chance from Monday to Thursday.

In the listing below, an approximate guide to current room rates (for a standard double room) is as follows:

€ = under €50
€€ = €50–90
€€€ = €90–140
€€€€ = over €140

In Bruges (Brugge)
Bauhaus International Youth Hostel
135–7 Langestraat
Tel: 050-341093; fax: 050-334180
www.bauhaus.be; e-mail: info@bauhaus.be
Good, youth-oriented budget accommodation with bicycle hire and launderette, close to the eastern ring canal park. €

't Bourgoensche Cruyce
41–3 Wollestraat
Tel: 050-337926; fax: 050-341968
e-mail: bour.cruyce@ssi.be
This is one of Bruges' gems, with eight rooms furnished in antique style; offers a perfect setting in the centre, and has an excellent restaurant. €€€

Central
30 Markt
Tel: 050-331805; fax: 050-346878
www.hotelcentral.be
e-mail: central@hotelcentral.be
Seven plain and simple rooms, with an enviable location on the Markt. €€

Dante
29a Coupure
Tel: 050-340194; fax: 050-343539
www.hoteldante.be
e-mail: info@hoteldante.be
A modern and stylish hotel, with a tranquil canalside setting and a good vegetarian restaurant. €€€

Duc de Bourgogne
12 Huidenvettersplein
Tel: 050-332038; fax: 050-344037
e-mail: duc@ssi.be
One of the most characterful hotels in Bruges, in a 17th-century canalside building. It stands in a picturesque position within easy reach of both the Markt and the Burg, and has rooms furnished in antique style and a good restaurant. €€€

Egmond
15 Minnewater

Tel: 050-341445; fax: 050-342940
www.egmond.be; e-mail: info@egmond.be
Plenty of atmosphere in a villa-style hotel
with gardens just beside the Lake of Love.
€€–€€€

Erasmus
35 Wollestraat
Tel: 050-335781; fax: 050-334797
www.hotelerasmus.com
e-mail: reservations@hotelerasmus.com
Nine nicely furnished rooms in a breezily
informal setting near the centre. **€€–€€€**

Fevery
3 Collaert Mansionstraat
Tel: 050-331269; fax: 050-331791
www.hotelfevery.be
e-mail: paul@hotelfevery.be
Has a good central position and delivers
good value for money. **€€**

Graaf van Vlaanderen
19 't Zand
Tel: 050-333150; fax: 050-345979
www.graafvanvlaanderen.be
A good budget choice, with a lively atmosphere; nightlife possibilities nearby. **€–€€**

Hansa
11 Niklaas Desparsstraat
Tel: 050-338444; fax 050-334205
www.hansa.be
e-mail: information@hansa.be
A modern hotel in an old house; breakfast
room still has decorated ceiling with chan-
delier. Rooms are small but good. **€€–€€€**

't Keizershof
126 Oostmeers
Tel: 050-338728
http://users.skynet.be/keizershof;
e-mail: hotel.keizershof@12move.be
Owned by an enthusiastic young couple who
make budget travellers welcome. **€**

Leopold
26 't Zand
Tel: 050-335129; fax: 050-348654
www.hotelleopold.com
e-mail: info@hotelleopold.com
Offers slightly more than budget-level
accommodation in a good location. **€**

De Markies
5 't Zand
Tel: 050-348334; fax: 050-348787
www.internetgids.be/demarkies
On the big square near the railway station,
this hotel is good value for money. **€€**

Montanus
76 Nieuwe Gentweg
Tel: 050-331176; fax: 050-340938
www.montanus.be
e-mail: info@montanus.be
A former budget hotel that has gone upmarket, with well-equipped rooms and an
expanded garden. **€€€**

Navarra
41 St-Jakobsstraat
Tel: 050-340561; fax: 050-336790
www.hotelnavarra.com
e-mail: reservations@hotelnavarra.com
A 17th-century royal residence, this hotel
treats guests like minor royalty; has an indoor
pool and a sauna. **€€€**

Passage
26 Dweersstraat
Tel: 050-340232; fax: 050-340140
Good, youth-orientated budget choice. **€**

Relais Oud Huis Amsterdam
3 Spiegelrei
Tel: 050-341810. Fax: 050-338891
www.oha.be; e-mail: info@oha.be
A lovingly restored 15th-century canalfront
building with lavishly furnished rooms. **€€€€**

Right: the Bauhaus Hotel in Bruges is a good option for youngsters on a budget

Rembrandt-Rubens
38 Walplein
Tel: 050-336439; fax: 050-336439
Minimalist facilities balanced by a friendly nature and genuine Old Bruges style. **€–€€**

Romantik Pandhotel
16 Pandreitje
Tel: 050-340666; fax: 050 340556
www.pandhotel.com
e-mail: info@pandhotel.com
An outstanding example of the Old Bruges style, with high-quality antique furnishings and a characterful location in an 18th-century mansion. **€€€–€€€€**

De Snippe
53 Nieuwe Gentweg
Tel: 050-337070; fax: 050-337662
e-mail: de.snippe@flanderscoast.be
Not far from the Begijnhof, this 18th-century hotel has atmospheric rooms and one of the best restaurants in Bruges. **€€€–€€€€**

Sofitel Brugge
2 Boeveriestraat
Tel: 050-449711; fax: 050-449799
www.sofitel.com
e-mail: h1278@accor-hotels.com
Spacious rooms and an atmospheric setting in a 300-year-old monastery just off bustling 't Zand square add to the character of this chain hotel. **€€€€**

Die Swaene
1 Steenhouwersdijk
Tel: 050-342798; fax: 050-336674
www.dieswaene-hotel.com
e-mail: info@dieswaene-hotel.com
Built around an 18th-century guildhouse, and with a great canalside position, this is a special place to stay. Its few rooms don't stay vacant for long, so it is best to book in advance. **€€€€**

In Damme
De Gulden Kogge
12 Daamse-Vaart Zuid
Tel: 050-354217. Fax: 050-371720
e-mail: gulden.kogge@planetinternet.be
This is a small country hotel with a notable restaurant and an enviable location beside the canal in Damme, just 6km (4 miles) from Bruges. **€€**

In Ghent (Gent)
Sint-Jorishof (Cour St-Georges)
2 Botermarkt
Tel: 09-224 2424. Fax: 09-224 2640
www.hotelbel.com/cour-st-georges.htm;
e-mail: courstgeorges@skynet.be
This hotel dating from 1228 claims to be the oldest lodging house in Europe, and its luxurious qualities and fine old style continue to attract. There's an equally noted in-house restaurant. **€€€**

Sofitel Gent Belfort
63 Hoogpoort
Tel: 09-233 3331. Fax: 09-233 1102
www.accor-hotels.com;
e-mail: h1673-hr@accor-hotels.com
Undoubtedly one of the best hotels in the city, with guaranteed comfort and a location close to the Belfry, right at the heart of things. **€€€€**

In Ostend (Oostende)
Danielle
5 IJzerstraat
Tel: 059-706349. Fax: 059-242390
www.proximedia.com/web/hoteldanielle.html;
e-mail: hotel.danielle@skynet.be
This mid-range hotel offers good-quality and fine modern facilities. **€€**

Oostendse Compagnie
79 Koningstraat
Tel: 059-704816. Fax: 059-805316
In a 19th-century royal villa this famous hotel right beside the beach retains a regal style, with luxurious rooms, sea views and tennis courts. Its Au Vigneron restaurant is highly regarded. **€€€**

Ypres (Ieper)
Regina
45 Grote Markt
Tel: 057-219006. Fax: 057-219020
At the heart of Ypres' rebuilt main square, the Regina is small and convenient enough to fill up quickly. **€–€€**

HEALTH & EMERGENCIES

Emergency services

Police *(politie)*, tel: 101

For non-emergency situations, the main police station is at Hauwerstraat 7, tel: 050-448844, and the Rijkswacht (Gendarmerie) headquarters is at Predikherenrei, tel: 050-447211.

Fire, tel: 100

Ambulance, tel: 100

Medical Services

Doctors: for doctors on weekend call (Friday 8pm to Monday 8am), tel: 050-813899.

Hospitals: Academisch Ziekenhuis Sint-Jan, 10 Riddershove, tel: 050-452111; Sint-Lucas Ziekenhuis, 28 Sint-Lucaslaan, Assebroek, tel: 050-369111.

Red Cross: tel: 050-320727.

Pharmacies: An *apotheek* is easily recognised by the Green Cross sign outside, and there are many scattered around town. Each one has a list on its door telling you where to find pharmacies that are open outside normal shopping hours.

Crime

This is not a worry in Bruges, though you can't entirely rule it out. As in any popular tourist area, it makes sense to keep an eye on your belongings.

Toilets

Public toilets are few and far between in the city, but you can use the facilities at many bars and restaurants provided you pay.

COMMUNICATIONS & NEWS

Post

The main post office is at 250 Markt, tel: 050-368597, and is open Monday to Friday 9am–6pm and Saturday 9am–3pm.

Telephone

The telephone area code for Bruges is 050, which (as with all Belgian telephone area codes) you must always use, even if you are calling a Bruges number from within the city. Most telephone boxes take telecards

of various denominations, which you buy at post offices, kiosks and newsagents; some boxes still take coins. To call the UK, first dial 00 44 then the area code minus the initial '0', then the subscriber number. For directory enquiries within Belgium, tel: 1207 or 1307; for international, tel: 1405.

Media

A Brussels-based English-language weekly news magazine, *The Bulletin*, is on sale in some Bruges newsagents, and has a good, Belgium-wide What's On section. The *International Herald Tribune*, as well as some British, Irish and other European newspapers are widely available. Cable and satellite television offers British and American networks, including BBC World, Sky News and CNN International. BBC Radio 4 can be picked up with near-perfect reception, as can the BBC World Service and Voice of America.

USEFUL INFORMATION

Disabled

Bruges is not notably access-friendly for travellers with a disability, though the fact that the city centre is largely pedestrianised simplifies matters greatly for wheelchair users. Bear in mind, though, that the streets are cobbled. Many museums have provision, and churches too can be easily entered. Public transport and canal boats are more problematic. Contact Toerisme Brugge, tel: 050-448686 for more details.

Children

Lots of things that appeal to adults in this beautiful city are bound to appeal to children. A canal-boat cruise, or a tour by horse-drawn carriage or horse-drawn tram surely fall into this category. Likewise, a return trip on the stern-wheel paddle steamer *Lamme Goedzaak (see page 84)* along the canal to nearby Damme, even if the pretty village itself hasn't much to offer them.

Children might also enjoy the marvellous view of the city from the 84m (272ft) Belfry *(see page 24)*, though climbing its 366 steps might not be so much to their – or your – liking (if you have a very small child who must be carried, bear in mind that the stairway is narrow, curving and steep, and often filled with people going up and coming down). The 47-bell carillon, whose mechanism is a fascinating thing to see in action, peals out every 15 minutes, and plays longer concerts several times a day in summer.

Art museums and churches filled with historic treasures will probably have a limited appeal. The Folklore Museum *(see page 40)* holds more promise, including the chance in summer to play some of the antique folk games of Bruges and Flanders. Not far from the museum is a cluster of windmills *(see page 41)*, several of which you can visit.

If you're in town on Ascension Day, the

kids should like to see the Middle Ages and biblical times brought to life in the Procession of the Holy Blood *(see page 78)*. Some children may enjoy seeing lace being made by hand at the Lace Centre *(see page 39)*. Similarly, the 'Bryggia My Love' multimedia show and the 'Brugge Anno 1468' medieval dinner show *(see pages 45 and 76)* help bring the city's history to life.

A big travelling fair with rides for all ages, plus fairground stalls and other attractions, is a frequent visitor to 't Zand square; check with Toerisme Brugge for the schedule. The vast range of amusements and the dolphin show at the **Boudewijnpark & Dolfinarium** (12 De Baeckestraat; tel: 050-383838; www.boudewijnpark.be; Apr–Aug daily 10.30am–6pm, Sept weekends 10.30am–6pm), in the southern suburbs, are a big favourite with children, and is an ideal trade-off for spending time trailing around Bruges' historic treasures with the adults. They can

let off steam on the rides and boats, and see the dolphins and the orca (killer whale). It's not unknown for adults to find that they, too, prefer the park.

Quieter thrills can be had at the **Zeven Torentjes Children's Farm**. A former feudal manor farm and estate dating from the 14th century in the eastern suburbs, at Canadaring, Assebroek, has been turned into a children's farm. There is also a blacksmith who demonstrates the old skills, including shoeing horses, and you can take free horse-and-carriage rides.

In summer, the excursion to Ostend *(see page 60)* is bound to be a favourite, for its excellent beach and safe bathing. It's not advisable to take children on a tour of the World War I cemeteries around Ypres , but they'll enjoy **Bellewaerde** (497 Meenseweg; www.sixflagseurope.com; May–Aug daily, Sept–Nov, Mar, Apr weekends and holidays; hours vary; tel: 057-468686 to check), an amusement park located in the once shattered landscape just outside the town *(see page 66)*. For adults, it stands as proof that life goes on.

Attractions

Many of the city's museums are listed in the various itineraries in this book. These other places of interest are in the environs.

Beisbroek City Park and Tudor City Park
Two adjacent big country estates in the forest southwest of the city, off Koning Albert I-Laan. The former has a Nature Centre (Apr–Nov, Mon–Sat 2–5pm, Sun 2–6pm; Mar, Sun 2–6pm), and a Planetarium (shows on Sun 3 and 5pm) and Observatory (Fri 8–10pm; Mar–Nov, also Sun 2–6pm). At the latter the splendid Tudor Castle has a classy restaurant and reception centre.

Castle of the Counts
The short trip to Male on the eastern fringe of the city is worthwhile for anyone interested in Bruges' history. Sint-Trudo Abdij (St Trudo Abbey, of the Sisters of the Holy Sepulchre) was once the castle of the counts of Flanders. Dating from the 12th century, it has been destroyed and rebuilt many times, but this vast moated castle-turned-abbey reflects the power and wealth of the Flemish rulers.

Lissewege

This engagingly pretty village north of Bruges on the road to Zeebrugge makes a great target for a cycling excursion or a short drive from the city in fine weather. There are handsome whitewashed old houses, and the Lisseweegs Vaartje, passing through the village, is a narrow canal that in medieval times connected it with Bruges. In the main square stands the huge, early Gothic Onze-Lieve-Vrouwekerk (Church of Our Lady), dating from 1225–50, with a flat-topped tower 50m (162ft) high, from which a carillon tune bursts forth occasionally. Inside, are a superb baroque organ, some interesting 17th- and 18th-century paintings, and a replica of a miraculous statue of the Madonna and Child destroyed by Dutch Protestants in the 16th century. The Historisch (Historical) Museum at 6 Walram Romboudtstraat displays archaeological finds from the area. Some of those concern the former Ter Doest Abbey, passed on the way from Bruges, which was destroyed by Dutch rebels in the 16th-century. All that remains is a remarkable Gothic barn from 1250, still used by the manor farm that replaced the abbey in the 1650s.

Sint-Andries (St Andrew's) Abbey

If you haven't had enough of the abbey habit in Bruges itself, visit this big Benedictine Abbey at Zevenkerken, outside Bruges to the southwest on Torhoutse Steenweg. Founded around 1100 and rebuilt in the 19th century after being destroyed by the French in the 18th, it is set amidst forests and makes a good side trip from the city. The monks produce fine pottery as well as icons. There is a popular cafeteria, the Benediktusheem, which serves cheap and cheerful food.

Tillegembos Provincial Estate

West Flanders Province's tourist office has set itself up in the Kasteel Tillegem (Tillegem Castle) at the heart of this splendid country estate southwest of Bruges, so if you want to see more of this part of Belgium you've come to the right place for information. The 14th-century castle is surrounded by a moat in which a pair of black swans glide, and a forested area that makes a pleasant place to walk.

Maps

Some hotels provide free maps that are a bit small but otherwise perfectly adequate. The pullout map in the wallet at the back of this guide plots all the itineraries in this guide.

LANGUAGE

The people of Bruges (and the rest of Flanders) speak Dutch. Behind this simple statement lies a thicket of complication. There is actually no such language as Dutch – the word reflects the historical inability of the English to distinguish between the languages (and peoples) of Germany *(Deutsch)* and the Low Countries *(Nederlands)*. To them it was all *Deutch*, which eventually corrupted into 'Dutch'. Many still consider – wrongly – that Dutch is the language of the Netherlands and Flemish is the language of Flanders. In fact, the language of the Low Countries, an area which encompasses both the Netherlands and Belgium, is *Nederlands*, not Dutch, and Flemish *(Vlaams)* is simply a local variant (not a dialect). It comes as something of a relief to discover that most people from Bruges speak good English.

SPORT

Olympiapark

If walking the length and breadth of Bruges hasn't been exercise enough, you can always visit this multipurpose sports centre at 74 Olympialaan. There's an Olympic-size swimming pool, a roller-skating rink, and facilities for tennis, squash and other sports. Bruges' two soccer teams, Club Brugge KV and Cercle Brugge KSV play at the complex's Jan Breydel Stadium.

USEFUL ADDRESSES

Tourist Offices

Bruges: Toerisme Brugge, 11 Burg, 8000 Brugge; tel: 050-448686; fax: 050-448600; www.brugge.be; e-mail: toerisme@brugge.be. Efficient and friendly, this office has a wealth of information on Bruges and the surrounding area, including maps, some of it

Right: parts of Bruges retain the ambience of a village

free and some with a price-tag. The staff will also help with accommodation and the office organises guided tours. It is open from April to September, Monday to Friday 9.30am–6.30pm; Saturday, Sunday and public holidays 10am–noon, 2–6.30pm; October to March, Monday to Friday 9.30am– 5pm, Saturday, Sunday and public holidays 9.30am–1pm and 2–5.30pm. Their free monthly *Exit* magazine and brochure *events@brugge* have information on current cultural and other events in the city.

Damme: Toerisme Damme, 3 Jacob van Maerlantstraat, 8340 Damme; tel: 050-353319; fax 050-370021; e-mail: toerismedamme@village.uunet.be

Ghent: Toerisme Gent Infokantoor, Belfort (Raadskelder), 17a Botermarkt, 9000 Gent; tel: 09-266 5232; fax 09-225 6288; www.gent.be; e-mail: toerisme@gent.be

Ostend: Toerisme Oostende, 2 Monacoplein, 8400 Oostende; tel: 059-701199; fax: 059-703477; www.oostende.be; e-mail: info@toerisme-oostende.be

Ypres: Toerisme Ieper, Lakenhallen, Grote Markt, 8900 Ieper; tel: 057-228584; fax: 057-228589; www.ieper.be; e-mail: toerisme@ieper.be

West Flanders province: Westtoerisme, Kasteel Tillegem, 8200 Sint-Michiels; tel: 050-380296; fax: 050-380292; www.westtoerisme.be; e-mail: westtoer@westtoerisme.be

This office provides information on the whole of the West Flanders province, including Bruges, Damme, Ostend, Ypres and the Belgian coast.

FURTHER READING

Insight Guides

The following are companions to this book:
Insight Guide Belgium, a combination of detailed and insightful reporting with a photo-journalistic style of photography, provides a comprehensive guide to the entire country,with a whole chapter on Bruges.
Insight Guide Brussels includes a chapter on Bruges as a sidetrip from the capital.
Insight Pocket Guide Brussels also includes an excursion to Bruges.
Insight Compact Guide Bruges is a mini-encyclopedia of the city.

Reference

Neat and square-shaped, *Treasures of Bruges* (Stichting Kunstboek, 1998) has 360 images and descriptions of paintings, sculptures and other works of art that you can see in the city's museums and churches.

To gain a detailed insight into all periods of the city's history, pick up a copy of *Bruges: Two Thousand Years of History* (Stichting Kunstboek, 1996).

Fiction

George Rodenbach's classic *Bruges-la-Morte* (Atlas Press, 1993), originally published in 1892, put the mouldering 'Dead Bruges' on the world's literary map.

Hendrik Conscience's *The Lion of Flanders* (Copernic, 1990), written in 1838, celebrates a great Flemish national epic – the Battle of the Golden Spurs victory over the French in 1302.

Also from Insight Guides...

Insight Guides is the classic series, providing the complete picture with expert and informative text and stunning photography. Each book is an ideal travel planner, a reliable on-the-spot companion – and a superb visual souvenir of a trip. 193 titles.

Insight Maps are designed to complement the guidebooks. They provide full mapping of major destinations, and their laminated finish gives them ease of use and durability. 100 titles.

Insight Compact Guides are handy reference books, modestly priced yet comprehensive. The text, pictures and maps are all cross-referenced, making them ideal books to consult while seeing the sights. 127 titles.

INSIGHT POCKET GUIDE TITLES

Aegean Islands	Canton	Israel	Nepal	Sikkim
Algarve	Cape Town	Istanbul	New Delhi	Singapore
Alsace	Chiang Mai	Jakarta	New Orleans	Southeast England
Amsterdam	Chicago	Jamaica	New York City	Southern Spain
Athens	Corfu	Kathmandu Bikes	New Zealand	Sri Lanka
Atlanta	Corsica	& Hikes	Oslo and Bergen	Stockholm
Bahamas	Costa Blanca	Kenya	Paris	Switzerland
Baja Peninsula	Costa Brava	Kraków	Penang	Sydney
Bali	Costa del Sol	Kuala Lumpur	Perth	Tenerife
Bali Bird Walks	Costa Rica	Lisbon	Phuket	Thailand
Bangkok	Crete	Loire Valley	Prague	Tibet
Barbados	Croatia	London	Provence	Toronto
Barcelona	Denmark	Los Angeles	Puerto Rico	Tunisia
Bavaria	Dubai	Macau	Quebec	Turkish Coast
Beijing	Fiji Islands	Madrid	Rhodes	Tuscany
Berlin	Florence	Malacca	Rome	Venice
Bermuda	Florida	Maldives	Sabah	Vienna
Bhutan	Florida Keys	Mallorca	St. Petersburg	Vietnam
Boston	French Riviera	Malta	San Diego	Yogjakarta
Brisbane & the	(Côte d'Azur)	Manila	San Francisco	Yucatán Peninsula
Gold Coast	Gran Canaria	Melbourne	Sarawak	
British Columbia	Hawaii	Mexico City	Sardinia	
Brittany	Hong Kong	Miami	Scotland	
Brussels	Hungary	Montreal	Seville, Cordoba &	
Budapest	Ibiza	Morocco	Granada	
California,	Ireland	Moscow	Seychelles	
Northern	Ireland's Southwest	Munich	Sicily	